C0-DXE-244

Clare of Assisi

Love's Reflection In The Window

17 Oct. 99

Carissimo Fr. Tim,

I wish you many blessings in your life of "giving" to our Lord and Lady! I look forward to getting to know you better.

Fraternally,

Br. Joseph

CLARE OF ASSISI

LOVE'S REFLECTION IN THE WINDOW

Robert Melnick, OFM CONV.
Joseph Wood, OFM CONV.

Mp
MARYTOWN
press

Marytown Press
LIBERTYVILLE, ILLINOIS

© 1995 MARYTOWN PRESS
1600 West Park Avenue
Libertyville, Illinois 60048-2593
708-367-7800
Fax 708-367-7831

Library of Congress Catalog Card 95-075987
ISBN 0-913382-65-5

Printed in the United States of America

To our Franciscan family throughout the world.

My beloved is like a gazelle,
or a young stag.
Behold, there he stands
behind our wall,
gazing in at the windows,
looking through the lattice.
My beloved speaks and says to me:
"Arise, my love, my fair one,
and come away;
for lo, the winter is past,
the rain is over and gone.
The flowers appear on the earth,
the time of singing has come,
and the voice of the turtledove
is heard in our land."

Song of Songs 2:9-12

CONTENTS

FOREWORD
Ramona Miller, OSF
xi

PREFACE
xiii

ENCLOSURE OF THE UNCONTAINABLE: A HISTORICAL REFLECTION
Joseph Wood, OFM CONV.
xv

LOVE'S REFLECTION IN THE WINDOW
1-67

PHOTOGRAPH REFERENCES
69

SAINT CLARE CHRONOLOGY
71

———■———

Foreword

DURING THE EIGHT HUNDREDTH ANNIVERSARY of her birth, Clare emerged from the shadow of Francis to be a radiant guide leading the way for those seeking soul satisfying meaning in life. Once a star led three Magi to Bethlehem where they found the infant Jesus in a stable. Today the star, "Chiara," guides us anew to our God "who was placed in a manger and wrapped in swaddling clothes" (4LAgl9). Clare lived the mystery of the Incarnation by humbling herself in imitation of Christ. Our renewed focus on her enclosed self-emptying has given birth to a new appreciation of Clare's message. As we move into the next millennium, countless faithful are reminded that contemplation is the source of wisdom and unending joy.

Assisi is an ancient city whose natural beauty evokes spiritual consciousness. Over the centuries, the visual harmony between the simple stone edifices, set on the rocky foothill of Monte Subasio, has maintained an atmosphere of tranquillity. The creators of this book captured exquisite photographs of this peaceful setting still graced by the abiding presence of Clare. Drawn into timelessness, the soul's eye is stretched beyond the horizons.

Clare taught Agnes of Prague a threefold manner of prayer: to gaze, to consider and to contemplate. She wrote, "gaze upon that mirror each day" (4LAgl5). This book initiates contemplative moments by providing visual images to gaze upon and poetic reflections to consider. The remembrance of Clare's life and writings nurtures the soul and generates love, leading us to "observe the poverty and humility of Our Lord Jesus Christ and of His most holy Mother" (RClXII, ll).

Yes, Clare leads us toward God. What a strange paradox! A thirteenth century noble woman, by faithfully embracing poverty out of love for the Poor Crucified Christ, sheds light on the shadow side of our lives. She stands as a lighthouse for modern seekers. May we follow her example and never tire of gazing upon Love Incarnate.

Ramona Miller, OSF

PREFACE

WE PRESENT THIS PHOTO MEDITATION as a complement to the many scholarly and creative endeavors that were part of the jubilee year, 1993-1994, celebrating the eight hundredth anniversary of the birth of Saint Clare. As Franciscans, we are enriched by the various new insights now being generated about this remarkable woman. In particular, we gratefully acknowledge that much of our narrative is developed from the recently published work, *Clare of Assisi, A Biographical Study*, by Ingrid Peterson, OSF.

Our book contains thirty-three "windows" drawing us into the world of Clare, a world of long ago in a valley where yesterday is today. Black and white photographs are used to highlight the interplay between illumination and shadow that has characterized life since the dawn of creation.

As we enter the story of "Chiara," a woman of light set upon the hill of human history, we also enter into the epic of God's endless passion for us. The language of the text reflects the spirituality of the Middle Ages—a time when hearts and imaginations were captured by romance, and communion with God was expressed as spousal love.

Robert Melnick, OFM CONV.
Joseph Wood, OFM CONV.

ENCLOSURE OF THE UNCONTAINABLE
A Historical Reflection
JOSEPH WOOD, OFM CONV.

"The aging world was almost oppressed by the weight of the years: the vision of faith faltering in the darkness, the footing of morals slipping away, the strength of virile deeds wanting; yes indeed, the dregs of the times were following those of vice; when God, the Lover of humanity, raised from the treasures of His kindness a newness of sacred Orders, providing through them both a support of the faith and a discipline for renewing morals. I would certainly say that these modern [founders] and their sincere followers were lights of the world, leaders of the way, teachers of life. In them the brightness of noonday dawned on a world at evening, so that *one who walks in darkness might see the great light.*"

Thus begins the eloquently poetic preface of the first official biography of Saint Clare, as commissioned by Pope Alexander IV at her canonization, August 11, 1255.

The eight hundredth anniversary of the birth of Saint Clare was officially celebrated between August 11, 1993–October 4, 1994. Up until this significant anniversary we were only seeing half of the story.

"Male and female God created them." We learned this lesson from the beginning in Genesis. The other half of the Franciscan story is feminine. The other half, which fulfilled the void in Francis' maleness, was the woman in his life.

Adam had Eve, Christ had Martha and Mary. John of the Cross had Teresa of Avila, Vincent de Paul had Louise. Francis had his Clare.

Often young people giggle to themselves when asking the proverbial question, "Did Francis and Clare love each other?" Naturally, they are alluding to a twentieth century type of love, including all the physical dimensions which that suggests. We usually respond, "Yes, Francis and Clare loved each other." They wait impatiently for the qualifiers. And the pause is just long enough for them to think that maybe qualifiers are not forthcoming. Somehow they begin to understand. Young and old need to hear that love is possible even for ordained and religious —and that we are not afraid to say so. From the beginning, God gave man and woman to each other. God said "Multiply" and never said "Stop." Love must be part of all of our lives. Love must radiate the reason for our religious choice of celibacy as well.

Before he died, Our Lord only asked one thing from weak humanity, "Remember me." The words haunt us. The Creator of life tenderly asked not to be forgotten. And so at every Eucharist, *we remember.* The anniversary celebrations of Saint Clare were also a call to *remember*, to remember the *whole* story: without fear, without qualifying any preoccupations that a male saint and a female saint saw in each other—dare we say it—love. A chivalrous love, a love from afar, an ideal love, a balanced love. Love.

For too many years we spoke of Francis without his Clare. To do justice to either a spiritual or scholarly pursuit of Francis or Clare, we simply cannot understand one without the other. And unfortunately, in the past when we spoke about the bond between Francis and Clare it had both a positive side and many drawbacks. Clare often appeared only as a reflection of her greater spiritual father. Francis was always the more active, the great preacher, teacher, miracle worker. Often, Clare even minimalized her role in his life by calling herself "the small plant of Francis."

Clare, of course, had a personality of her own. She was a woman of initiative and courage. Because she was a born aristocrat—and throughout her life was always referred to as *Lady Clare*—one would think she would have had a life of ease and privilege, even greater freedoms than her frivolous middle class counterpart. It is true Clare's family was the wealthiest, most powerful in Assisi. But in reality, although Clare was better educated than Francis, she was not better pampered.

In the first Scripture reading from the feast of Saint Clare, Hosea, the Old Testament prophet, speaks about a lady coming from a desert exile where she has been strengthened, a lady who will espouse righteousness and justice. How appropriate an image when recalling the life of Lady Clare. Because of civil war between the nobility and the rising merchant class after the assassination of the Holy Roman Emperor, Henry VI, all of Italy was in upheaval. The nobility were thrown out of Assisi quite violently when Clare was about six years old. Clare spent her youth as an exile in the city of Perugia, the mortal enemy of Assisi. She lived among relatives and strangers who sided with the enemy city in order to win back Assisi at whatever cost. Although not personally participating, her family was responsible for the death of many Assisi citizens who merely wanted to govern themselves in a democratic fashion. Unlike Francis, Clare's life was not filled with the music of the troubadours or the carefree luxury of daydreams.

After returning from exile years later, when the nobility won the upper hand, Clare often heard Francis preaching in the cathedral. And after listening to the wonderful stories of the community life of the friars from her cousin, the Count Rufino, a shy and gentle man who had recently given up everything to follow Francis, Clare decided to do the same. On Palm Sunday in 1212, she left her family to follow Francis. Robing herself in a great cloak she smuggled her way through the city gates in the middle of the night. It was not the momentary whim of a foolish and spoiled eighteen year old girl. She knew what she was seeking, she knew what she was rejecting.

Francis gathered his brother friars at the small chapel, Portiuncula, in the forest below Assisi, where they anxiously awaited the arrival of Lady Clare. As was the ritual, Francis cut her hair as a statement of her renunciation of the world. Although awed by her strength of will and determination to give herself totally to God, Francis was remiss at what to do. A tonsured woman could not live with tonsured men. Therefore, Francis at first placed Clare with the Benedictine sisters in the town of Bastia, not far from Assisi. But that soon proved to be unacceptable. Clare believed that God called her to begin something new for women, as God had called Francis to begin something new for men.

She who was noble, remained noble. Clare soon proved to her well-intentioned *Knight of Poverty* that she was a member of the ruling class not merely because of her ancestry but because of her tenacity of spirit. She knew what she could accept and she knew what she could not live without. She knew what God wanted. She knew what she wanted. There was no alternative.

We may ask ourselves, "Could Clare not have resigned herself to life in a Benedictine abbey with other holy women? Could she not have resigned herself to reforming whatever needed to be reformed in that ancient Order? Could she not have been satisfied in doing God's will by simply being a good nun no matter where she was?"

In order to understand such questions we must first appreciate some of the religious customs of the Middle Ages. A noble woman could enter a convent if her family permitted it, instead of making an advantageous marriage, but usually the girl would take her dowry with her. She would take valuable furniture as gifts. The family would also offer lands to the monastery as well as serfs to work the land. The young woman would even take one or two family servants who would also become nuns—extern sisters—in order to wait on her and perform the ordinary duties of running a castle-like convent. Also, because local violence was not uncommon, Benedictine abbeys always maintained an appropriately sized garrison of men-at-arms, usually under the direct authority of the abbess.

Clare shatters the religious traditions of her society. She takes no dowry, she takes no servants, she takes no gift of furniture or land, she wants no garrison surrounding her cloistered walls.

Francis was soon compelled to take the Lady Clare to a new convent, the convent he had unknowingly prepared seven years earlier: San Damiano, the small church Francis rebuilt with his own hands, was that sacred place where he heard the voice from the crucifix commission him, "Go and rebuild my Church." There was no other place more suitable. And while they walked to San Damiano, did the thought not enter their chivalrous minds: *How else could one rebuild a living organism—the Church—without a loving male and female partnership?*

Once in her own convent, Clare continues to break with tradition, even with the very governing structures of religious life. Unlike Benedictine abbesses who lived removed from the nuns, Clare slept in the common dormitory with her sisters. Her place in the refectory, sitting among her sisters instead of presiding at a head table, expressed her desire to serve rather than be served. Clare introduced universal suffrage, the right for all the sisters to vote regarding convent decisions. She, who was single-minded in telling the man who inspired her that she would not live in a Benedictine abbey, was, however, unafraid of sharing authority and responsibility with the other women in her life. Clare was the first woman in the history of the Church to write a Rule for women. Her ideal of poverty and trust in God was so radical that the pope agonized over approving her Rule until the hour of her death, when finally, he personally presented it to her in the convent dormitory where she died the very next day.

How could Francis not have loved the Lady Clare? As a woman she was gentle and tender, caring for him in his last illness after his eyes had been cauterized. But as a woman in a man's world, she was also dynamic, challenging, innovative. She was a leader of women, an advisor to men. She always said "yes" to God, but sometimes said "no" to human authority. How could Francis not have wanted to be near her, even though it sometimes made him a little nervous? How often did Francis call out to Brother Angelo, a former knight, a man who shared the same chivalric ideals as he, "Come, let us go visit the Lady Clare." How often did Francis remind his brother friars that if they wanted to see *Lady Poverty, Lady Chastity, Lady Obedience*—personified images of the virtues—they would find them all residing in the person of Lady Clare. "Look to her when I am no longer with you," he admonished. Francis, the fanciful man who danced in the sunset while rubbing two sticks together pretending to play the violin, was still a man who needed concrete expressions in his life. The Lady Clare was his constant model even when his brothers argued over policy and necessary practical development.

Clare became a new light for a tired generation. She reminded her people of the need for God in their lives. She also reminds us of the constant need for contemplation, for renewal, for striving to return to ideals. Our age, too, has become "oppressed by the weight of the years."

The only answer for suffering humanity's longing desires and willing hands is the example of the Lady Clare—the example of prayer. Because Clare was aware of suffering and injustice throughout her life, she left the world in order to transform it. The cloister became her pulpit, her tilled garden became her battlefield of interior reform.

A young Poor Clare sister explained the contemplative ideal best when speaking to a university group who asked about the seeming futility of a life behind walls. "But if I leave the monastery," she said, "I would only be in Assisi. If I stay within the cloister, I am in the entire world." Nothing else needed to be said. The students were beginning to understand the enigmatic wisdom of the long contemplative tradition within their Church. Cloistered men and women are often more aware of world events than we who are *in the world*. Contemplatives are continually praying for or listening to people coming to their doors sharing their stories. Maybe that is why another pope named a contemplative sister, Therese of Lisieux, the Little Flower, Patroness of the Missions.

In 1255, two years after Clare's death, Pope Alexander IV commissioned one of the most poetically elegant documents in the history of the canonization process. To announce her entry into eternal glory, the pope played with the image of light, a symbol more comprehensible when learning that Clare's name in the original Italian is *Chiara*—lady of light.

While this light remained certainly in a hidden enclosure, it emitted sparkling rays outside. Placed in the confined area of the monastery, yet it was spread throughout the whole world. Hidden within, she extended herself abroad. In fact, Clare was hidden, yet her life was visible. Clare was silent, yet her reputation became widespread. . . . let the multitude of saints rejoice because *the nuptials of a new royal bride* are being celebrated in their heavenly midst.

Our busy world desperately needs a light to redirect the path of social development. Saint Clare reminds us that the only sure foundation we have is God's radiant presence in each of us. This divine light gives life to our interior cloistered garden. Yet, our garden only flourishes when we till the soil with the cross, and patiently tend the growth by pruning it with Gospel values.

Reprinted with the permission of *Companion* magazine, Box 535, Station F, Toronto, Ontario, Canada M4Y 2L8.

Clare of Assisi

Love's Reflection In The Window

At a time when the world had grown cold,

when the pursuit of wealth and power

wrapped humanity in an icy pall of indifference

toward God and others . . .

———■———

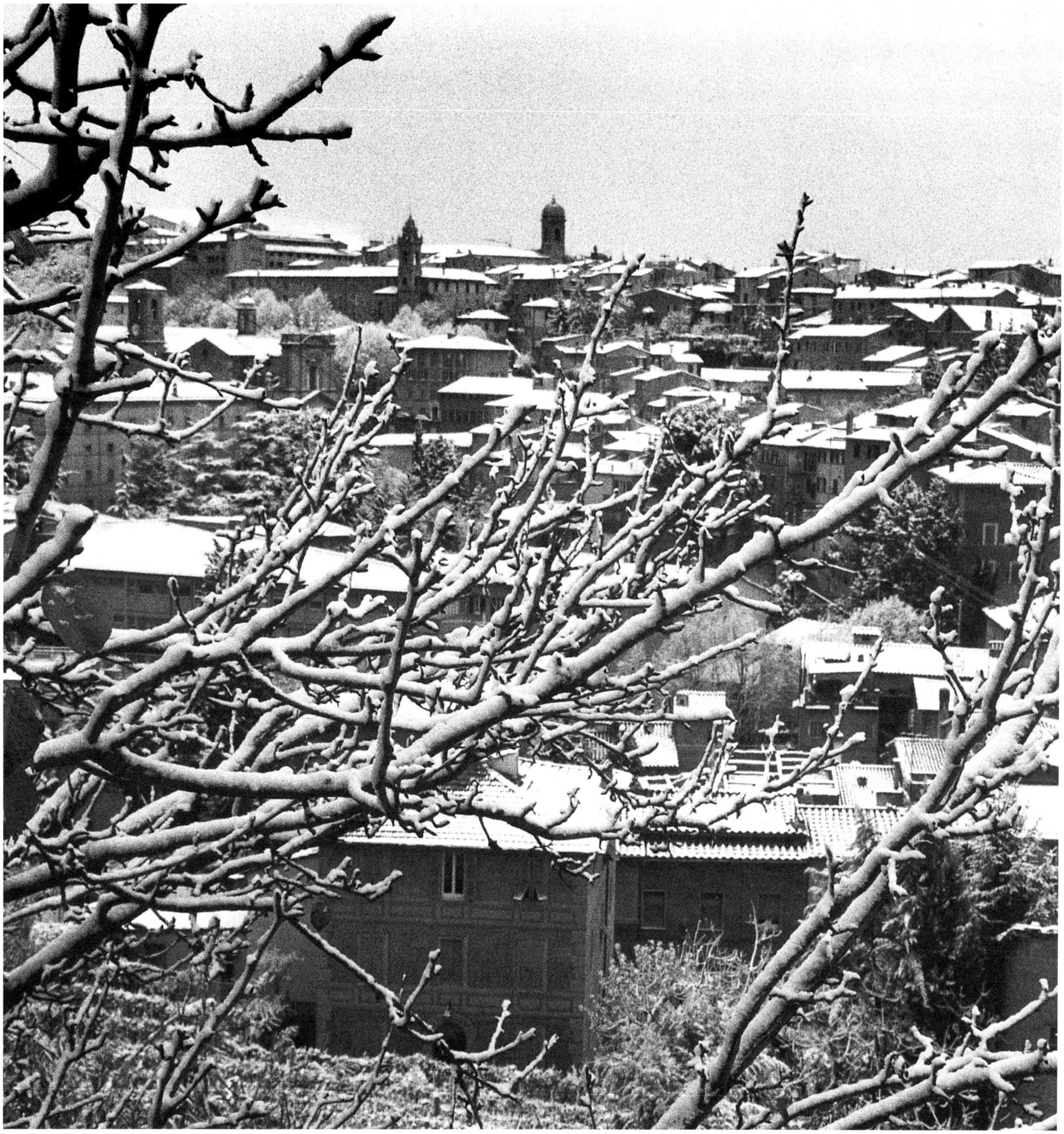

3

At a time when the guiding light of the Church

was dimmed by the gathering gloom of a lost generation,

a people trapped in the shadow of forgotten ideals . . .

———■———

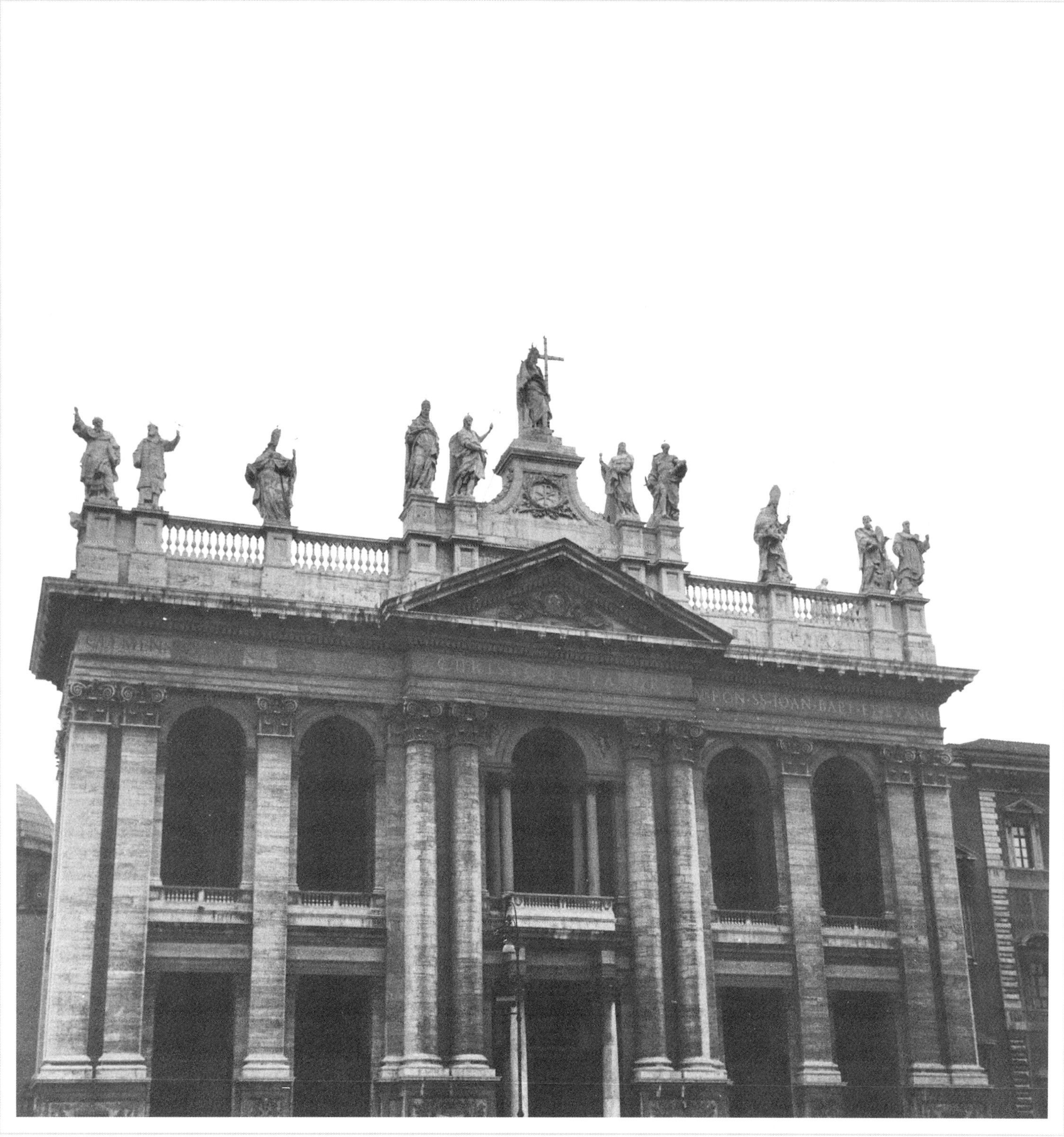

At a time when the people of God had abandoned the light of Christ . . .

God did not abandon the people.

Divine mercy permeated the darkness of the ruling class

and planted a new seed of illumination.

A prophecy announced to Lady Ortulana of Assisi that she was to

"give birth to a light that will shine brilliantly in the world."

And so it happened.

In the year 1193 we were given Clare,

"noble by birth but nobler still by grace."

———■———

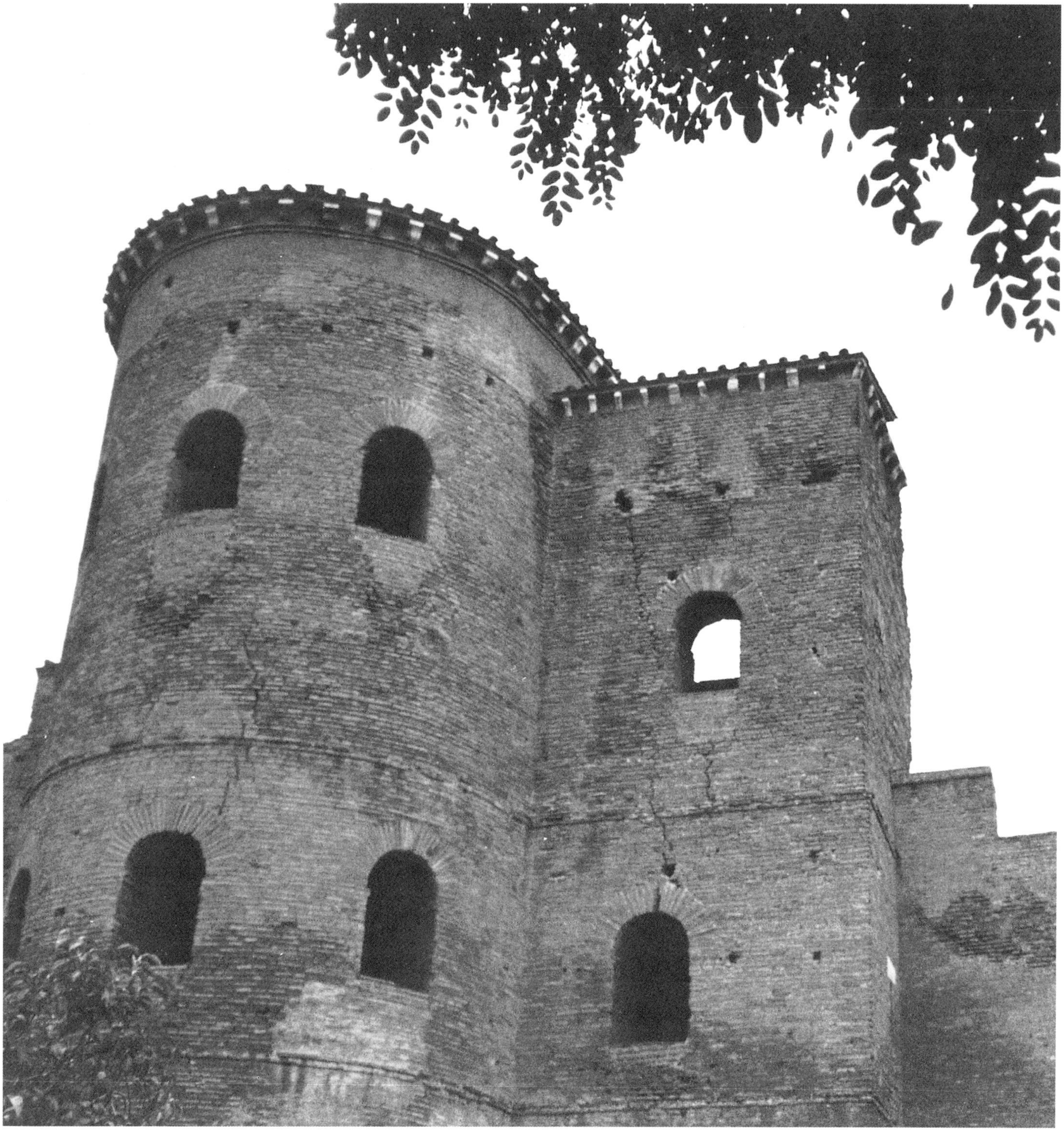

Though privileged with the status of her family,

Clare was nurtured in Christian love by her faithful mother.

Thus, even as the glowing coals of animosity between the classes

left a dark residue of hatred on the social order,

Clare became a lamp of sanctity in troubled Assisi.

Her "manner of living was angelic, kind, humble, compassionate,

even when she was just a small child."

───■───

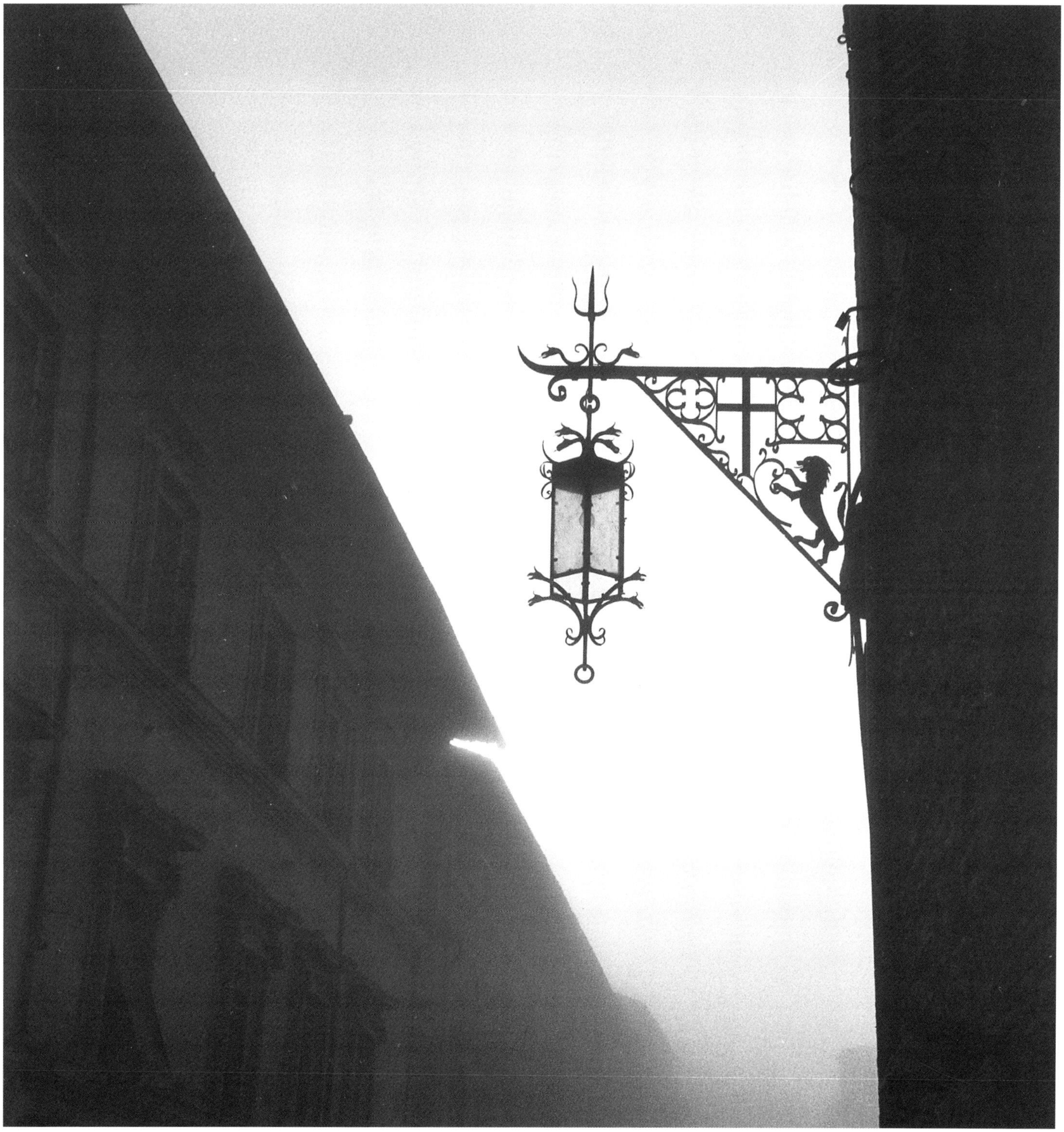

Yet evil persisted.

Cruel violence was taken up as a sword

by the commoners slaying the oppressive system,

and as a shield by the nobles battling to maintain power.

Smoldering tensions exploded into such terror

that the noble women and children fled to Perugia.

There, Assisi's bitter foes conspired

with the ousted noblemen

to quell the revolution.

———■———

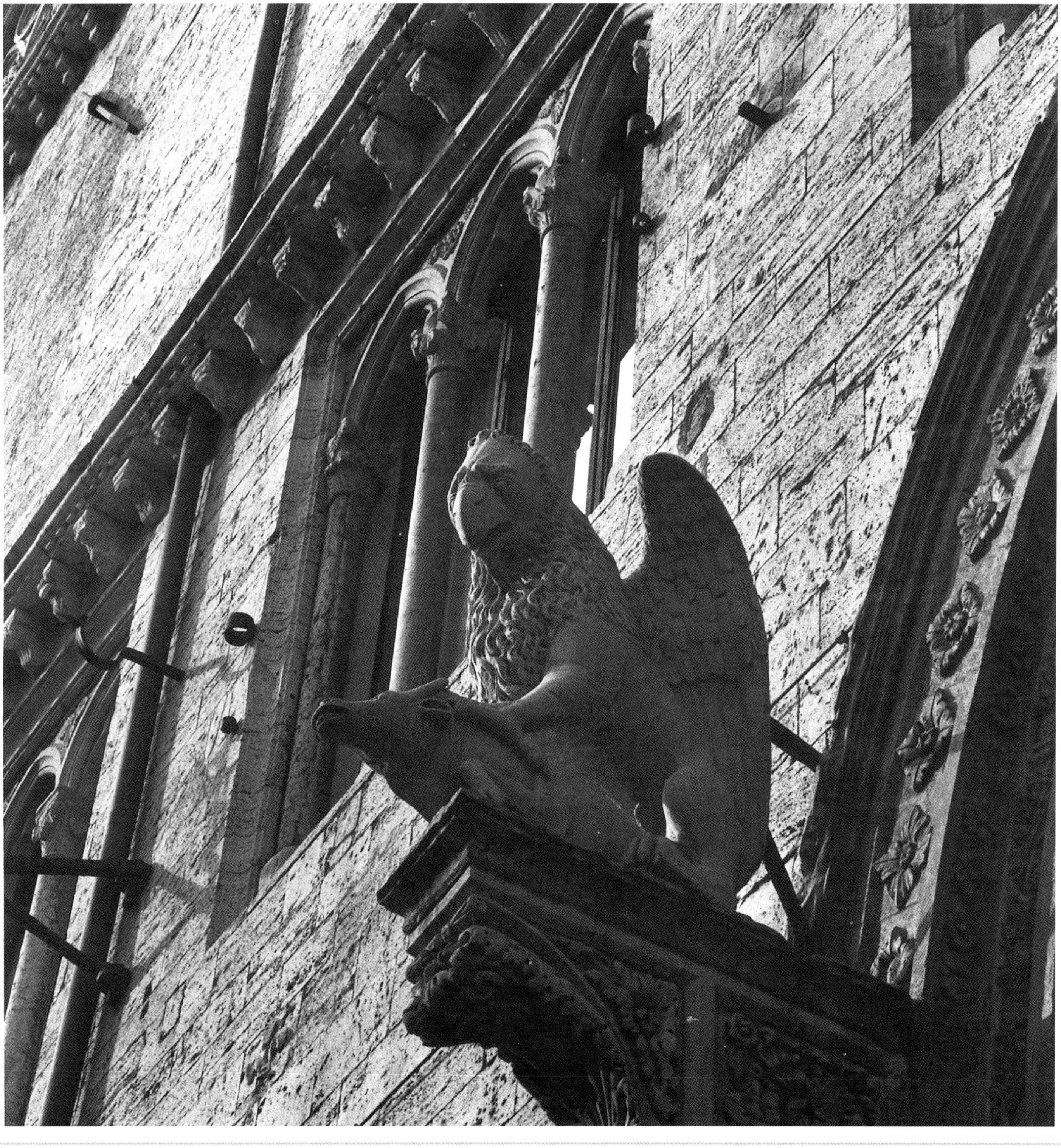

Uprooting Clare from her birthplace,

exile was a harsh gardener for her blossoming youth.

Far from being a peaceful paradise,

Perugia was a city choked by weeds of contempt.

Its walls echoed with cries of war

and clashes of weaponry.

Clare longed for her home,

but she grew to realize that home was not a place,

home was a relationship with Love itself.

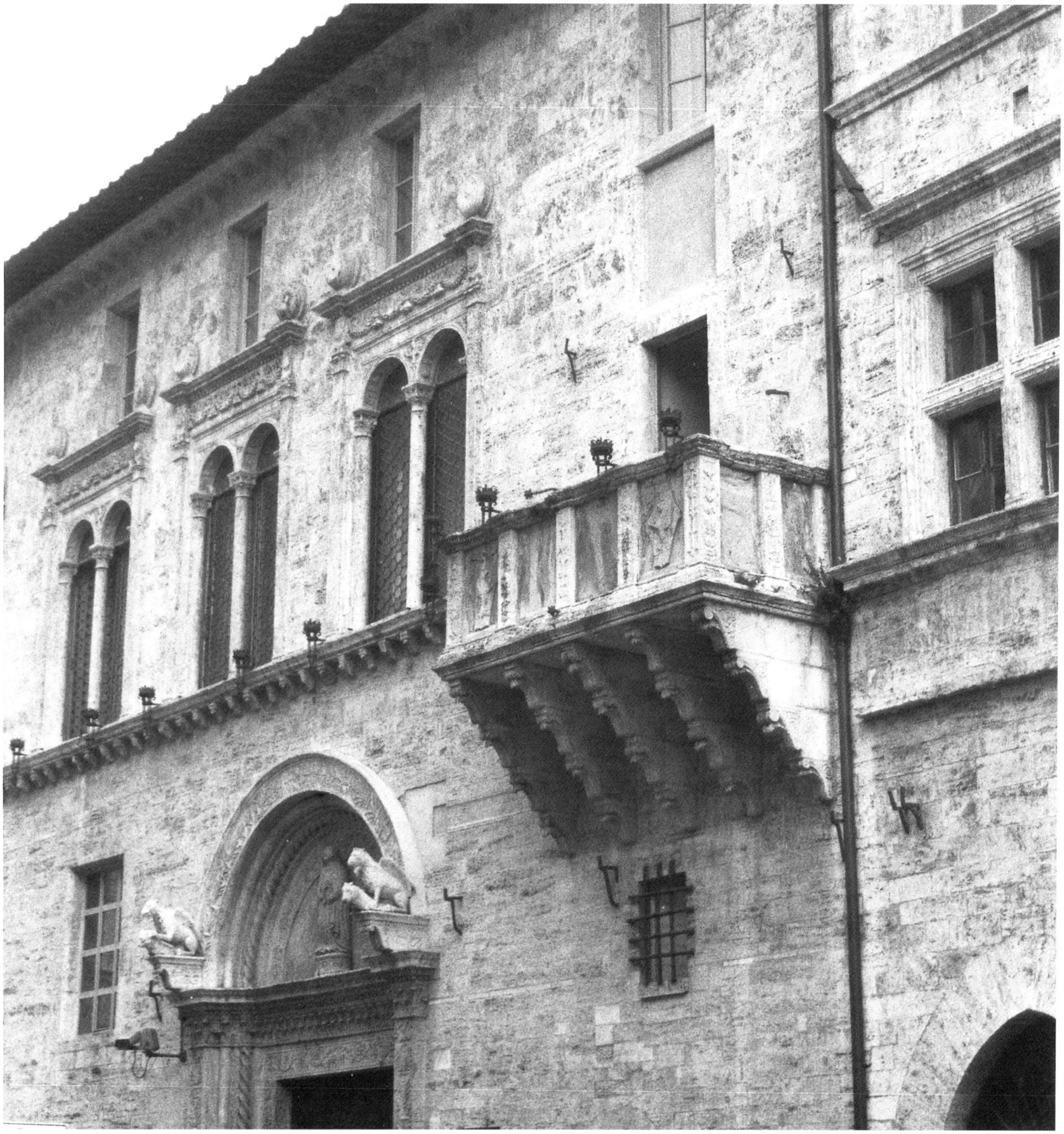

Love had drawn Clare into its living waters at baptism.
Love had filled her with an inner spring of grace
that flowed over in acts of faith.
And it was Love that inspired Clare
to help repair the broken spirit of Assisi upon her return.
Hence, she contributed human goodness instead of material goods,
she patronized spiritual banquets rather than lavish feasts,
and she chose royal virginity over noble marriage.

———■———

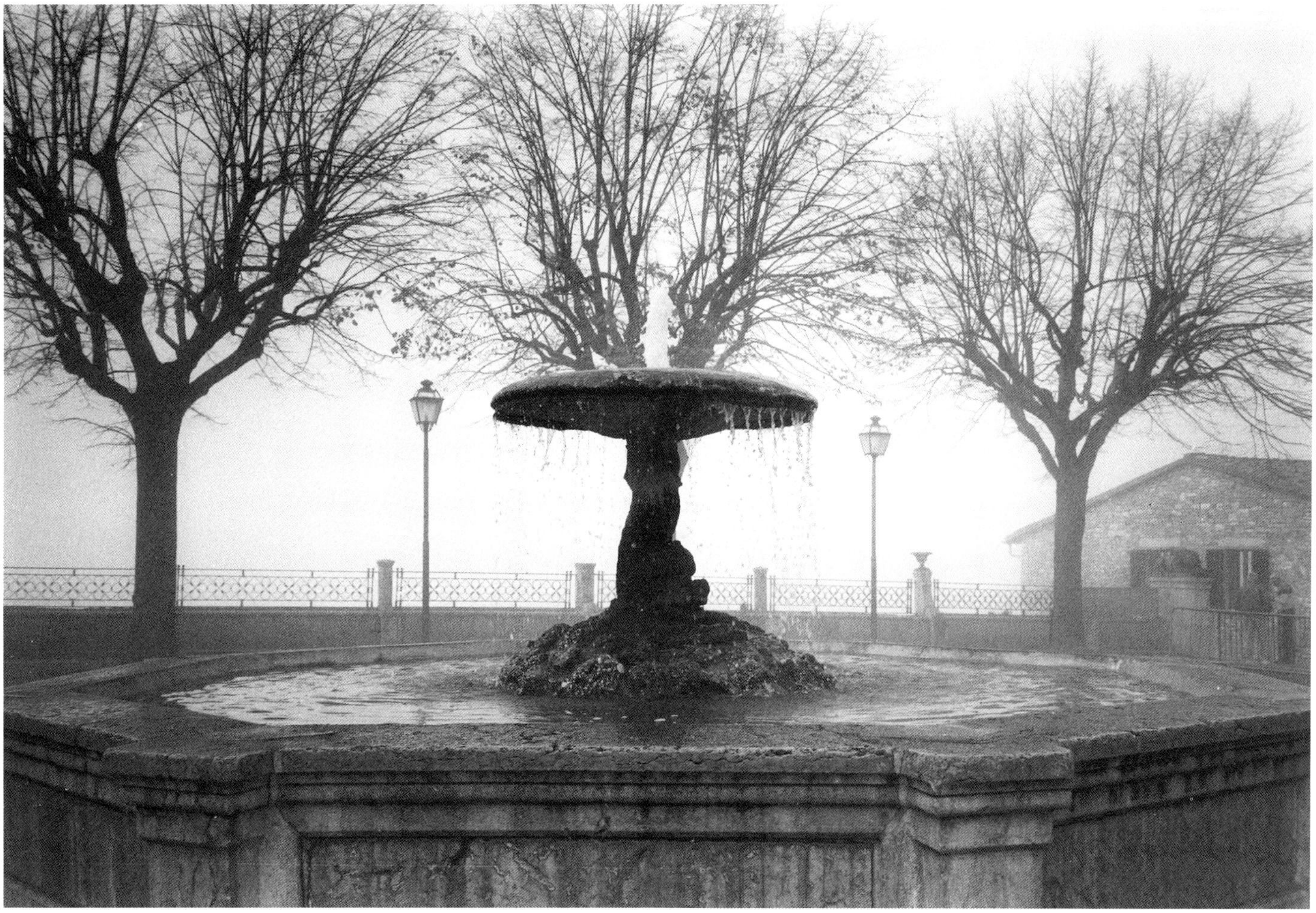

After years of prayer and penance

in the company of the women of her household,

Clare was a radiant young lady passionately in love with Jesus.

Mature in faith and stature, she was now ready

for a fuller union with the Son of God.

Their courtship began as Clare encountered Francis di Bernardone

preaching in the cathedral.

He who was an incarnation of the Incarnate One

was enchanted by the spiritual beauty of this noble woman.

———■———

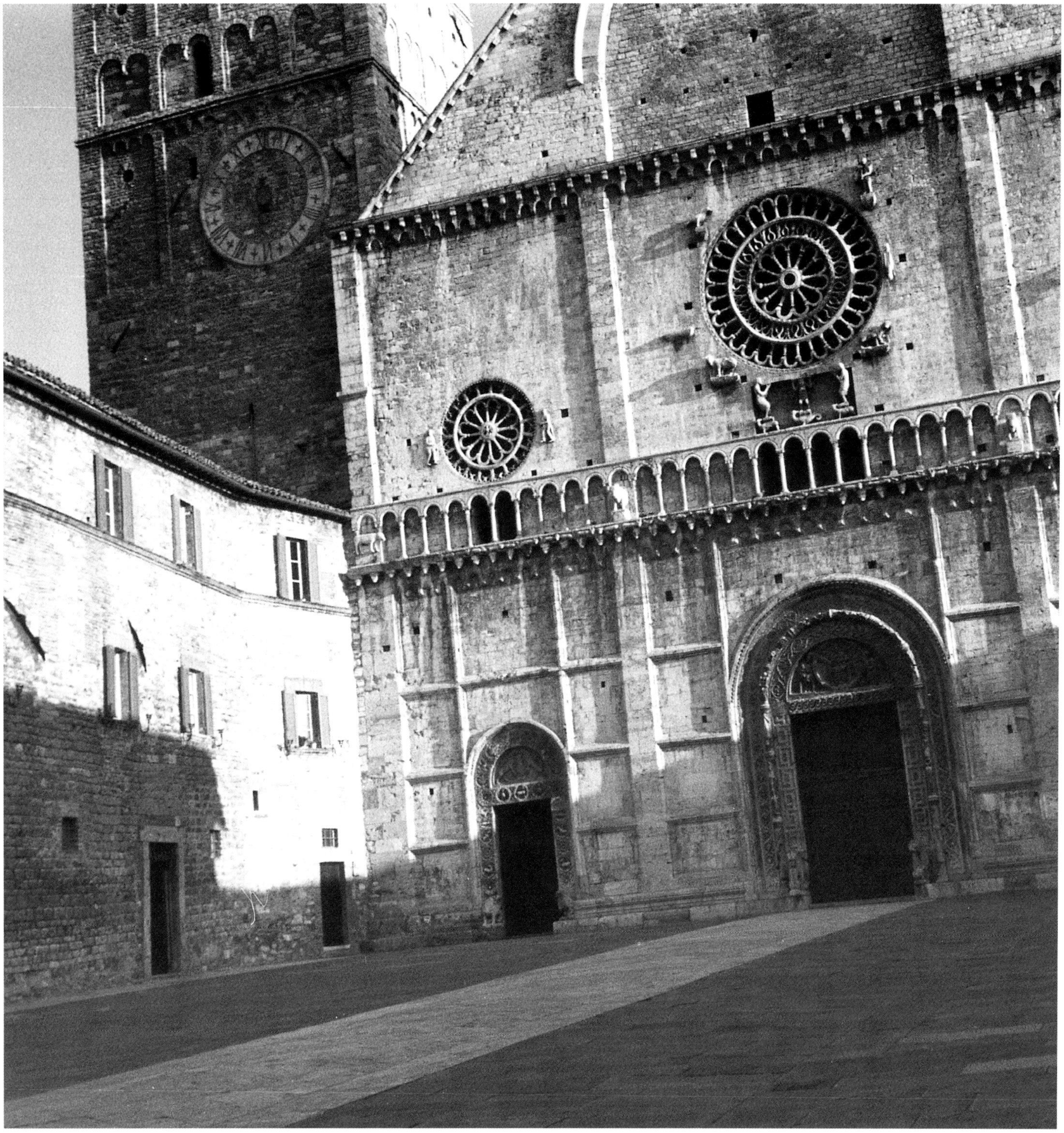

For two years Clare and Francis met secretly.

Acting on behalf of his Lord, Francis animated the Gospel

to intensify the light of devotion shining in Clare's heart.

It became clear that her expansive love could no longer be contained

by the restrictive structures of medieval life.

Clare knew she had to forsake her familiar surroundings

in order to fully embrace her true love,

the Body of Christ.

———■———

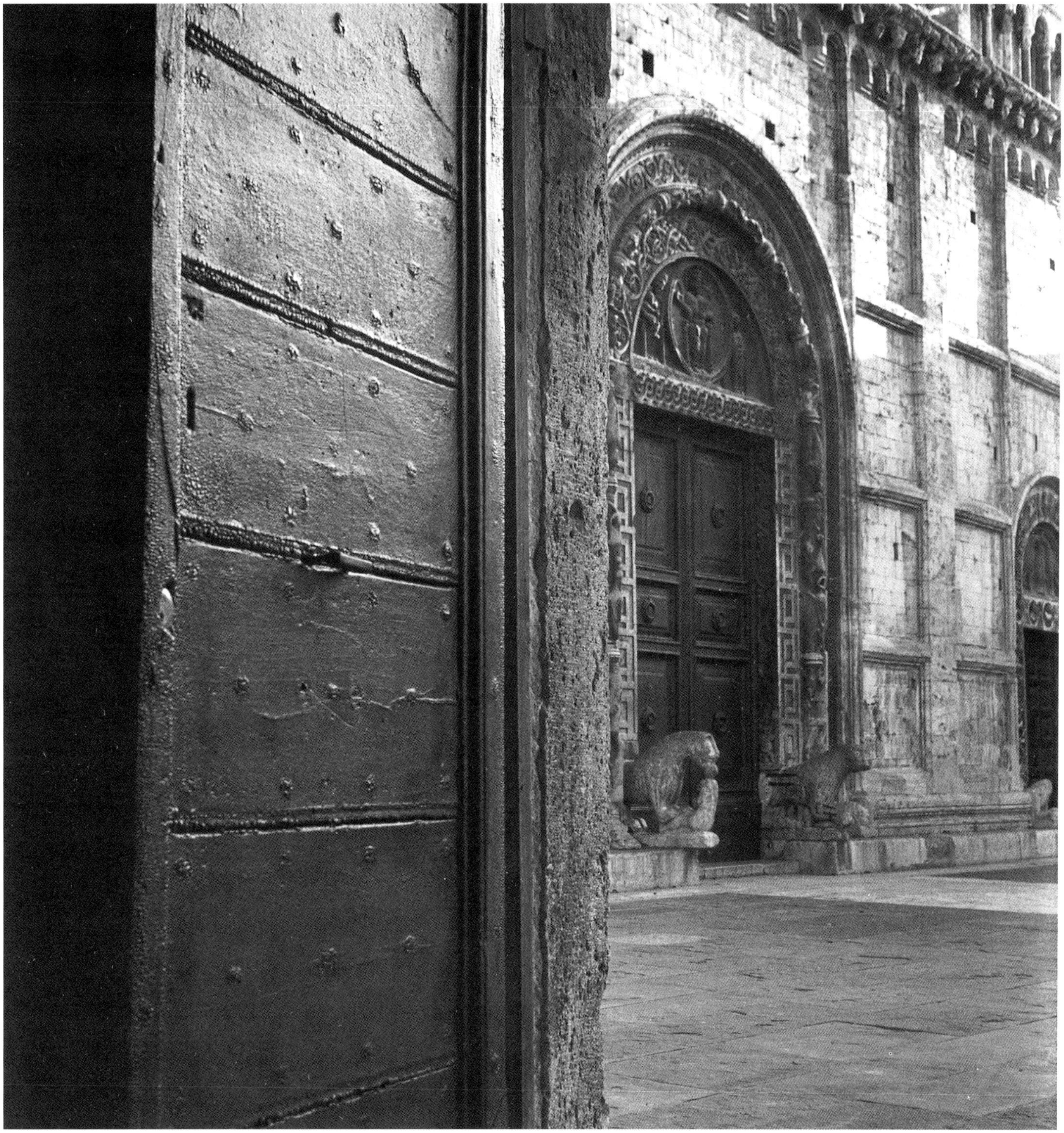

It was Palm Sunday in the year 1212.

Eighteen year old Clare boldly descended the summit of her social rank

to espouse the Prince of Poverty.

Going forth under the cloak of night,

Clare's way was lit by the resplendent gown of virginity

and the glittering jewels of virtue

she wore as her dowry.

———■———

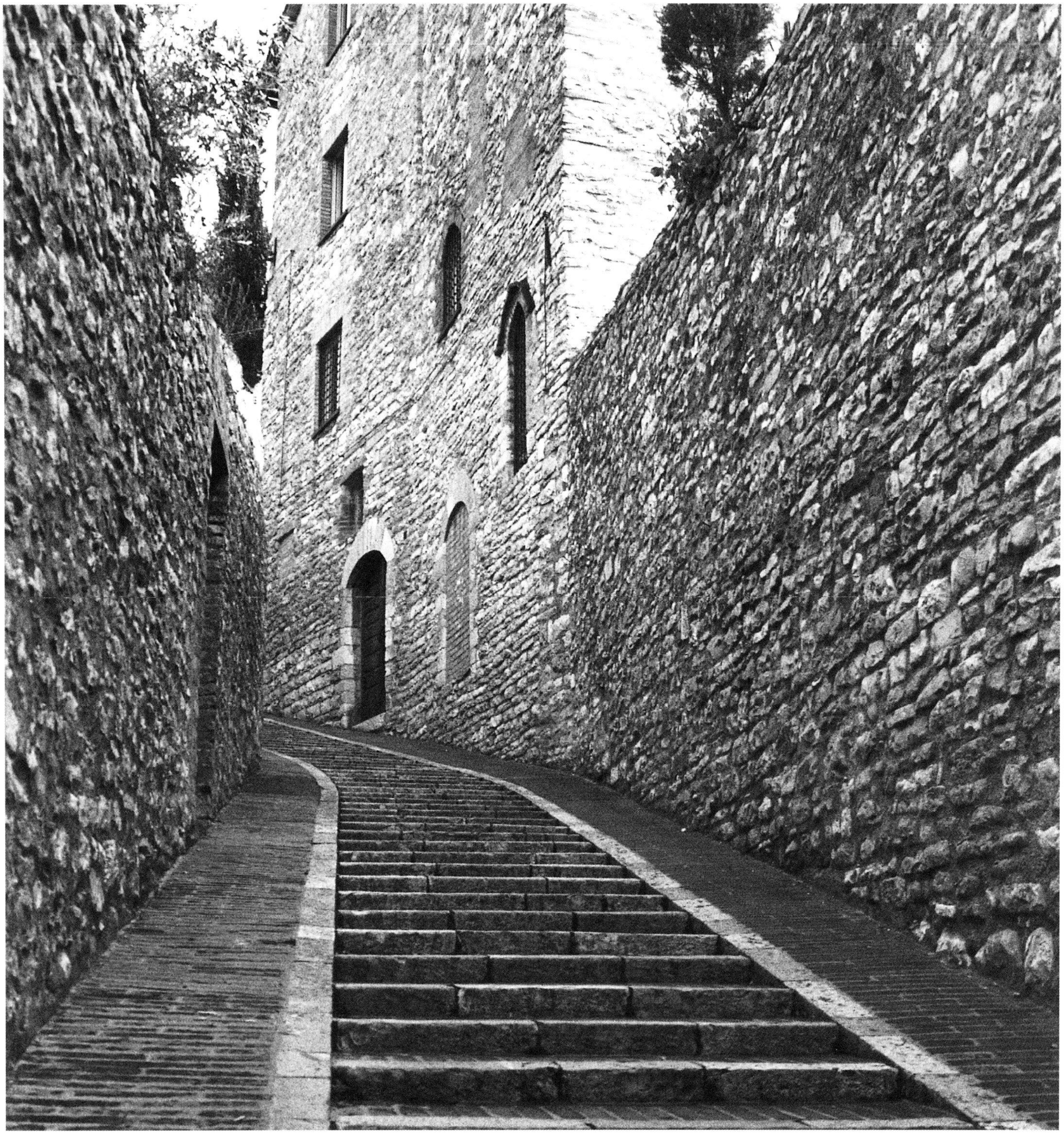

In an act of absolute trust,

Clare left security behind as she went through the city gate.

Her passover was complete:

no longer a lady protected by the walls of aristocracy,

Clare became a woman vulnerable in the thick forest

that lay between her past and her future.

———■———

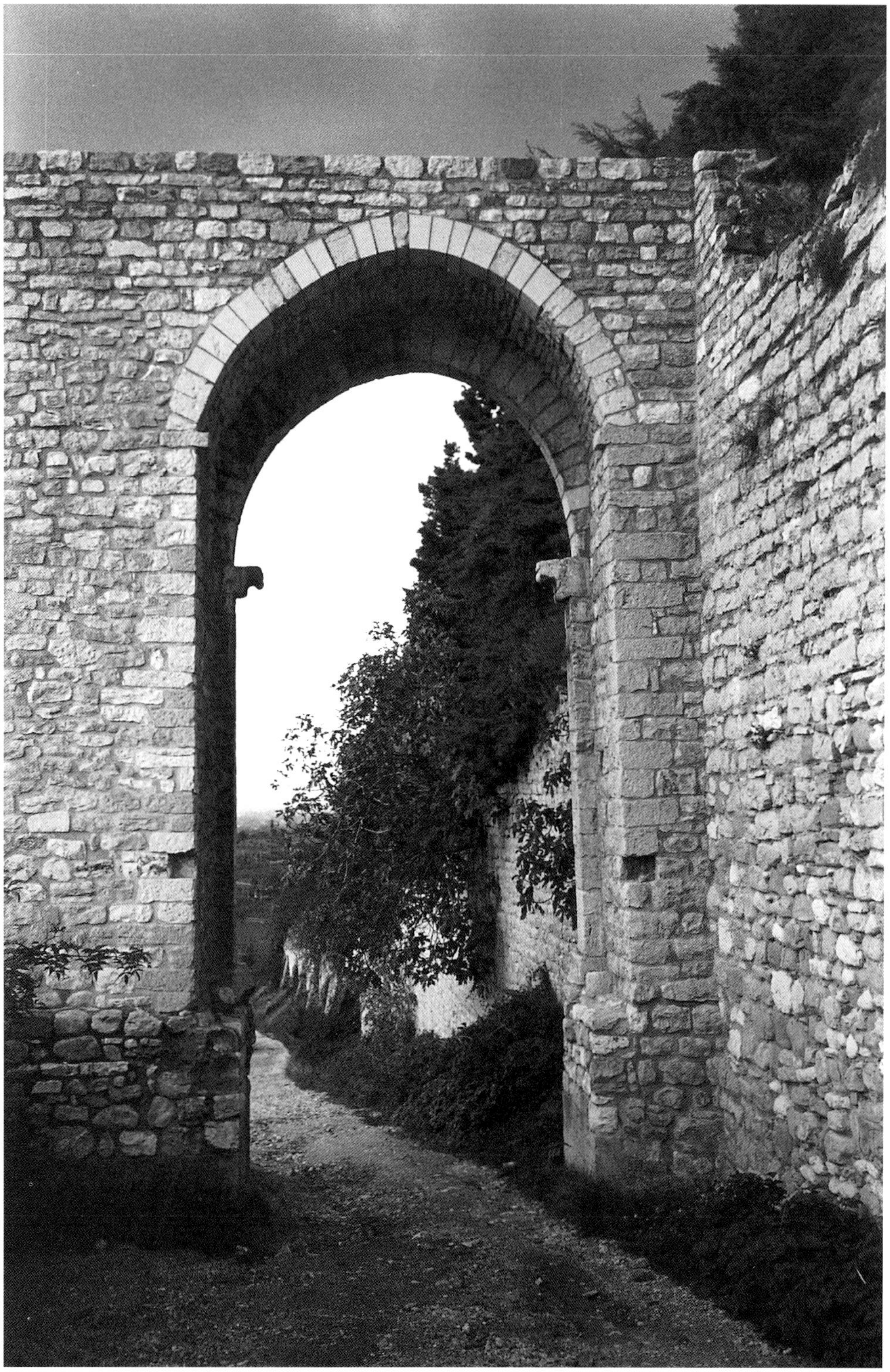

The Light of the World beckoned and

Clare hastened to meet her Lover.

Though the road was familiar,

her bridal path was untrod.

No woman had ever surrendered herself to Christ

in the same way as the virgin Clare.

───■───

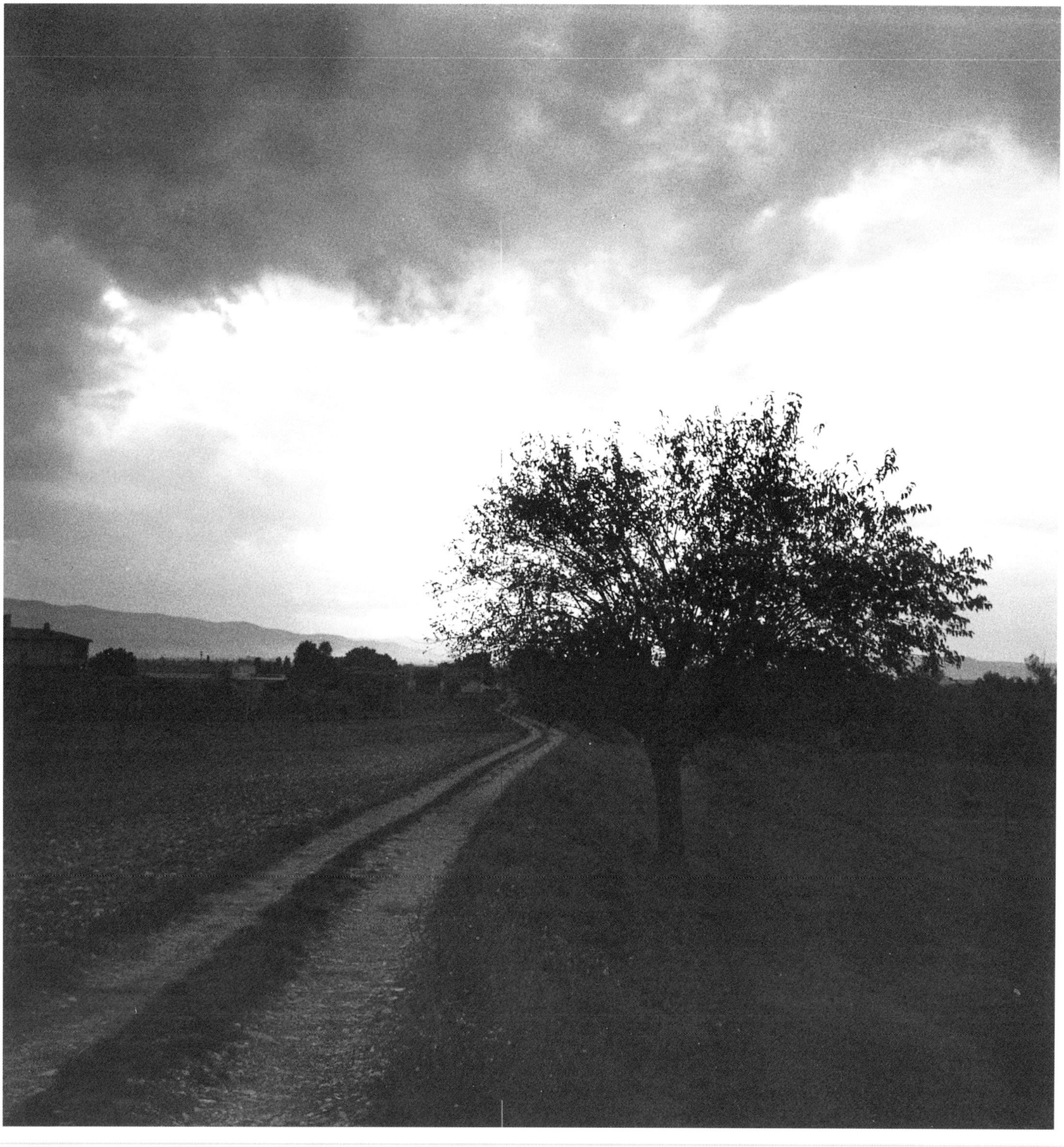

The guests were attired in the finest robes of ragged poverty.

The banquet of sacrifice was prepared.

Arriving at the Portiuncula,

the anxious bride joyfully gazed on her intended spouse.

Herself arrayed in sparkling holiness,

Clare's groom was stripped in humility.

Her wedding procession, her way of the cross,

brought Clare ever closer to the promise of ecstasy

in the arms of the Crucified,

in the arms pierced by passion waiting to embrace her.

───■───

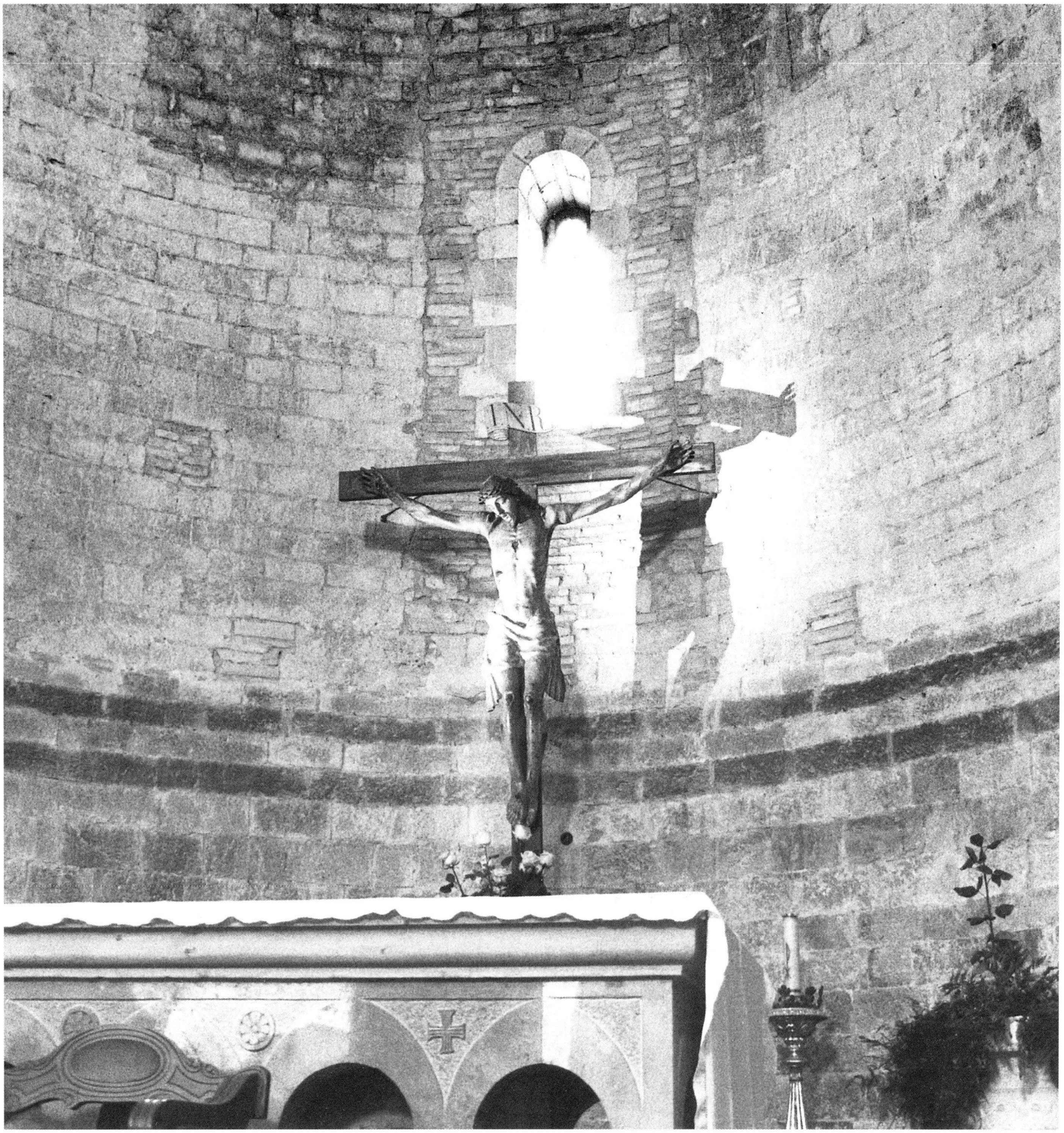
INRI

Francis presided at the nuptial ceremony

in which Clare pledged to love, honor and cherish

the poor Crucified all the days of her life.

The covenant was sealed as Francis clipped away

the golden tresses of Clare's hair, the pride of her maidenhood.

And, as she became one with Christ,

Clare's poverty, chastity and obedience

brought sustaining strength to the union.

———■———

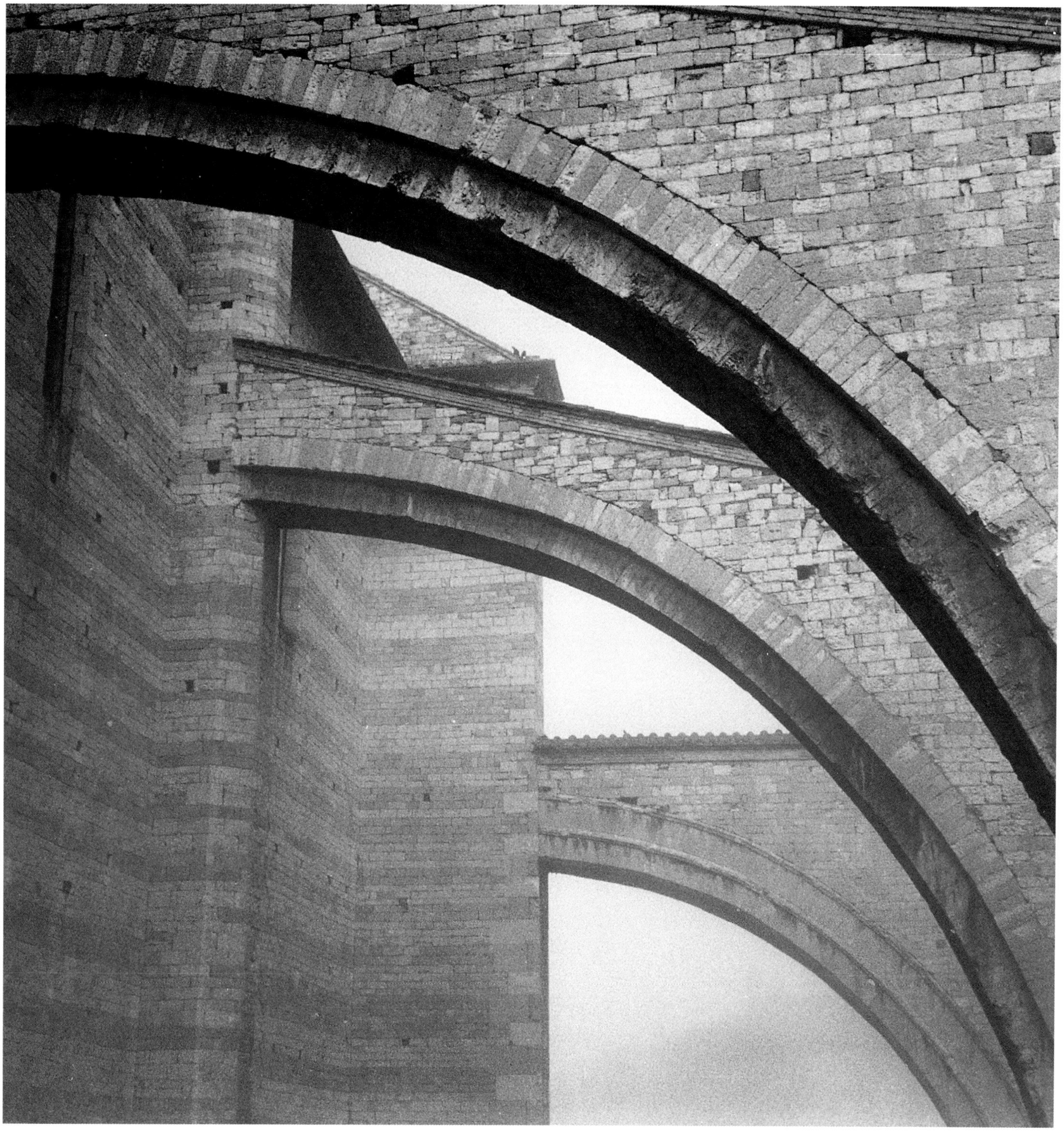

Still, this mystical marriage was immediately imperiled

by the indignant fury of Clare's family.

Enraged by the sudden elopement of a woman expected to

marry into political and economic alliance,

Clare's uncle Monaldo and his fierce knights

stormed the monastery that sheltered her.

Intent on recovering his loss,

Lord Monaldo erupted with venomous threats

as Clare thwarted his attack

by clinging to the sanctuary of the altar.

———■———

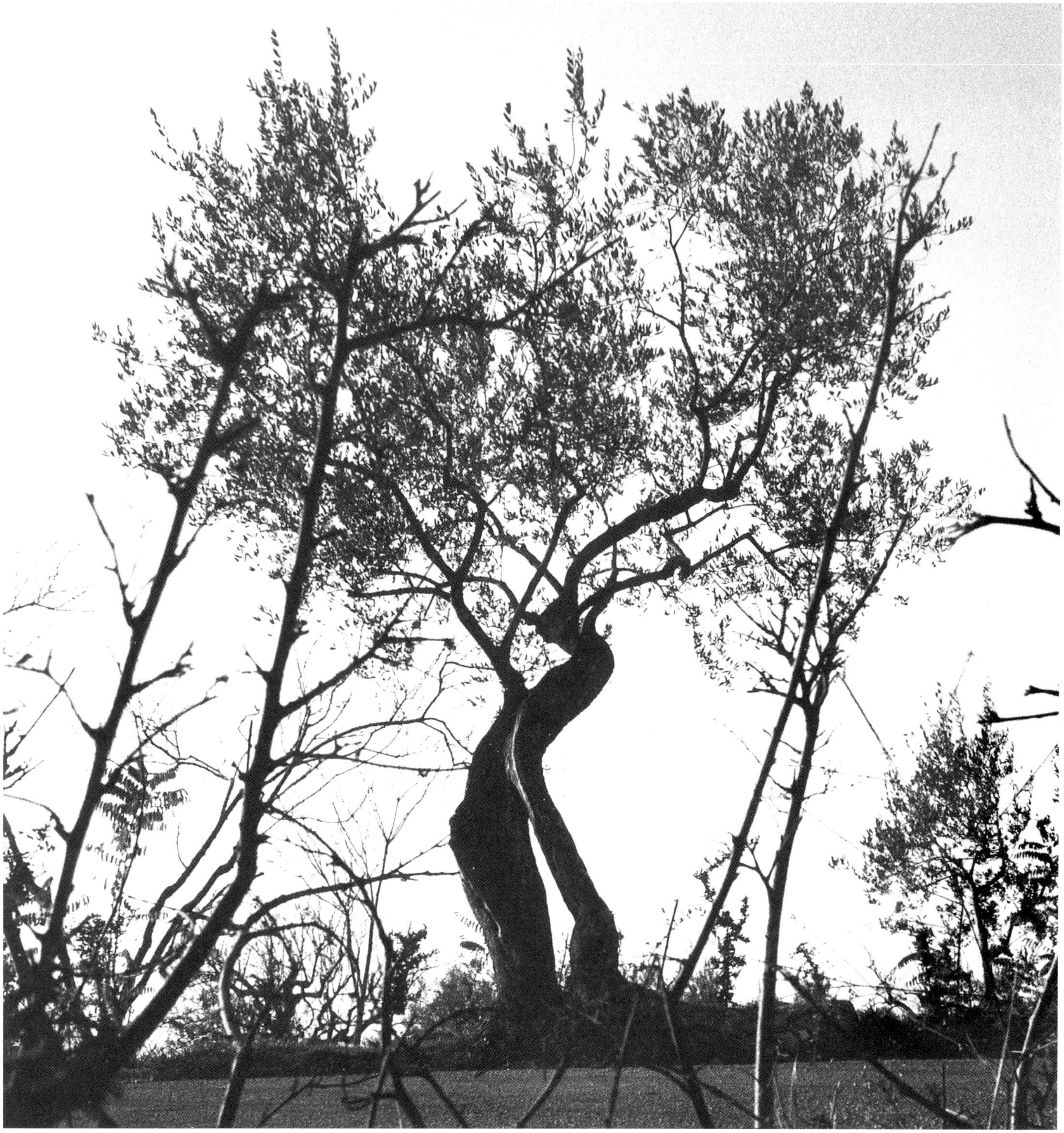

Vanquishing Assisi's knights of power

through her tenacious night of prayer,

Clare remained with her beloved outside the walls of conformity.

And soon the fiery pillar of Love,

which had already consumed Clare,

began to engulf other hearts as well.

Clare's sister Agnes became the first of many noble women

who made a daring exodus into the Umbrian wilderness.

———■———

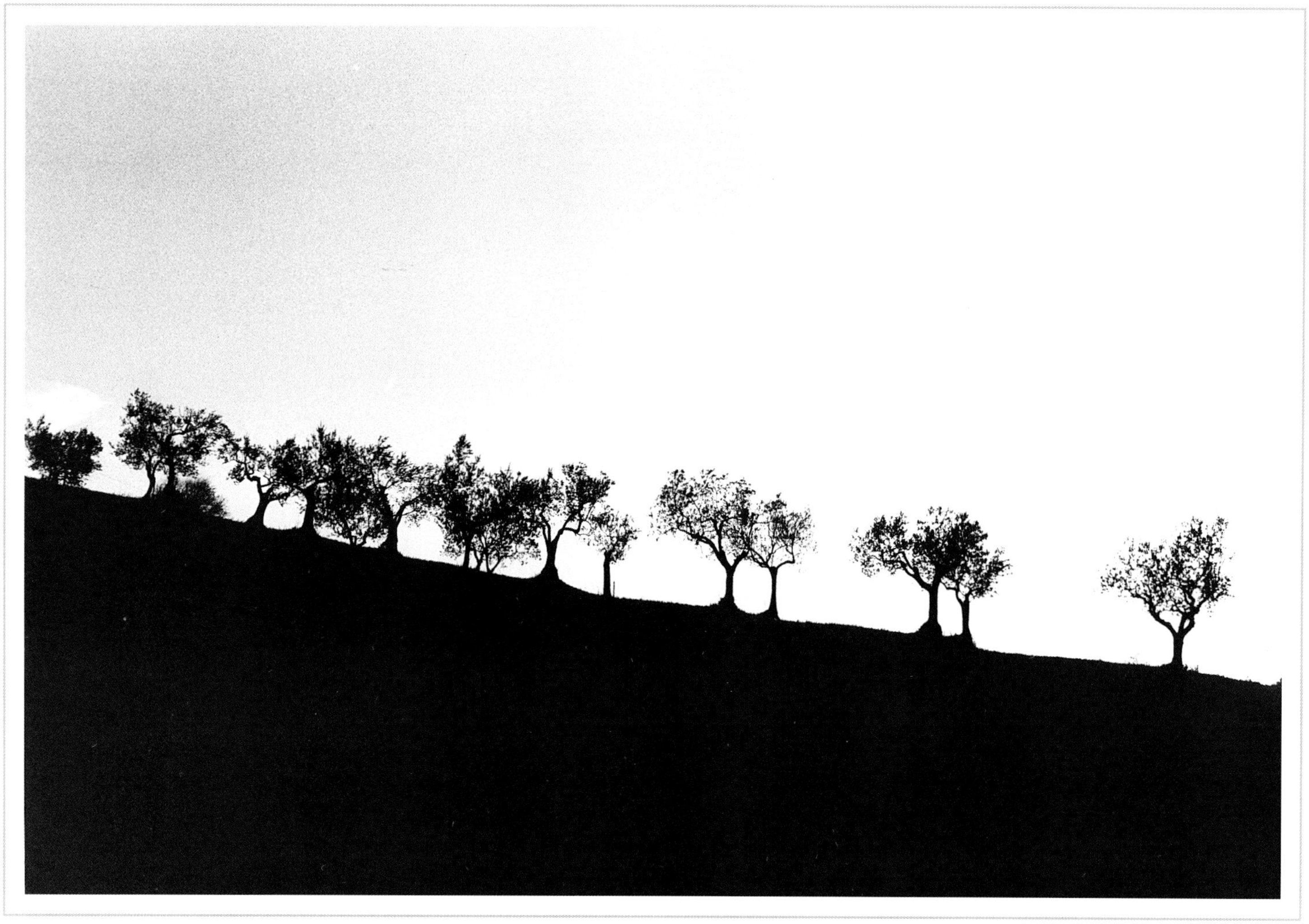

The hardships of their inner pilgrimage toward Love

penetrated these brave women with the mystery of Christ Crucified.

Enveloped by the Passion of her spouse, Clare assured her sisters that,

"If you suffer with Christ you will reign with Him.

If you weep with Christ you will rejoice with Him.

If you die with Christ on the cross of tribulation

you shall possess heavenly mansions in the splendor of the saints

and in the Book of Life your name shall be glorious among all."

———■———

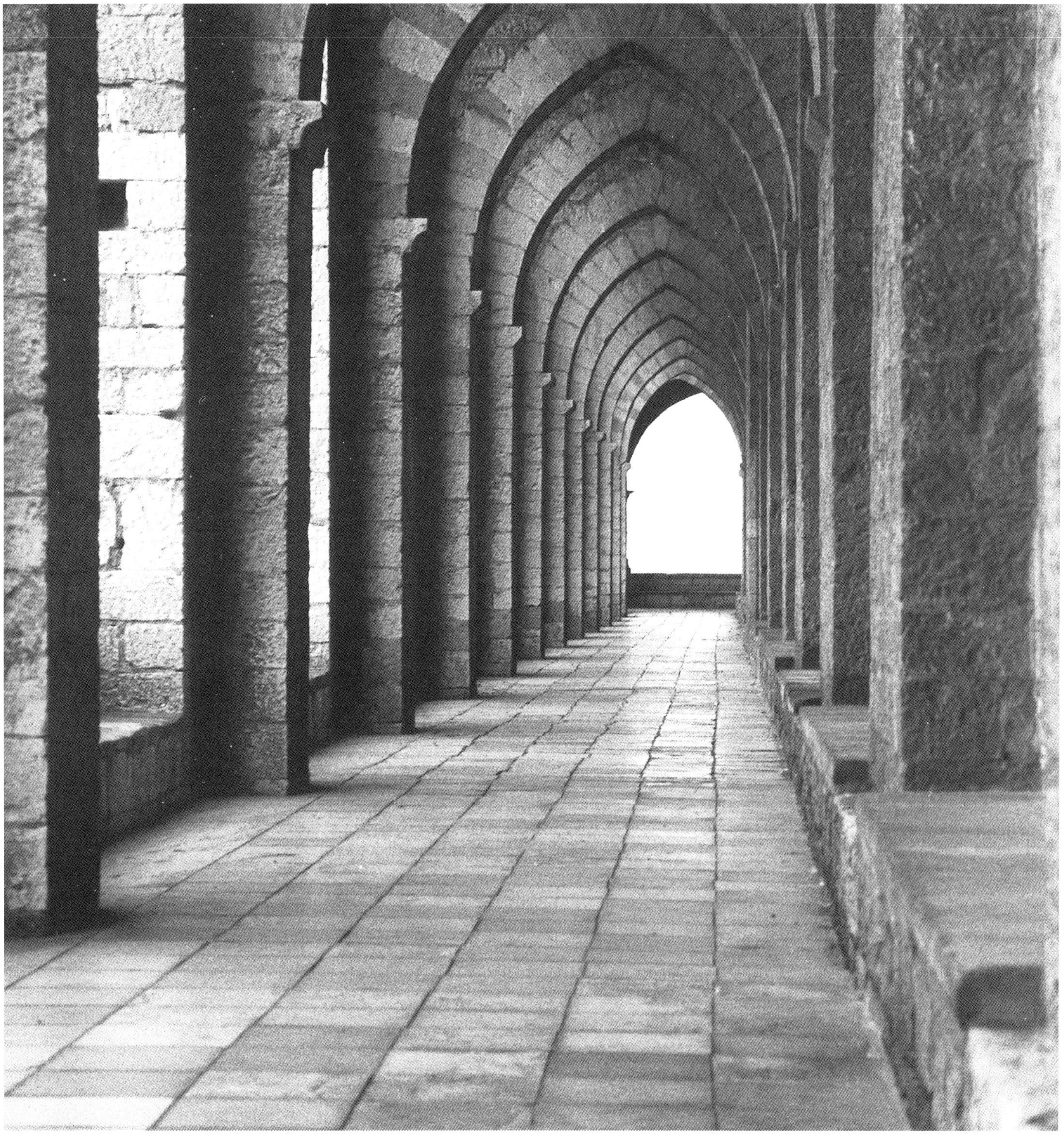

Gradually the young brides living at San Damiano

began to experience deep intimacy with Christ through frequent prayer.

Clare urged her companions to discover the fullness of Love

by basking in divine light as living icons of God.

"Place your mind before the mirror of eternity!

Place your soul in the brilliance of glory!

Place your heart in the figure of the divine substance!

And transform your whole being into the image of the Godhead itself

through contemplation."

———■———

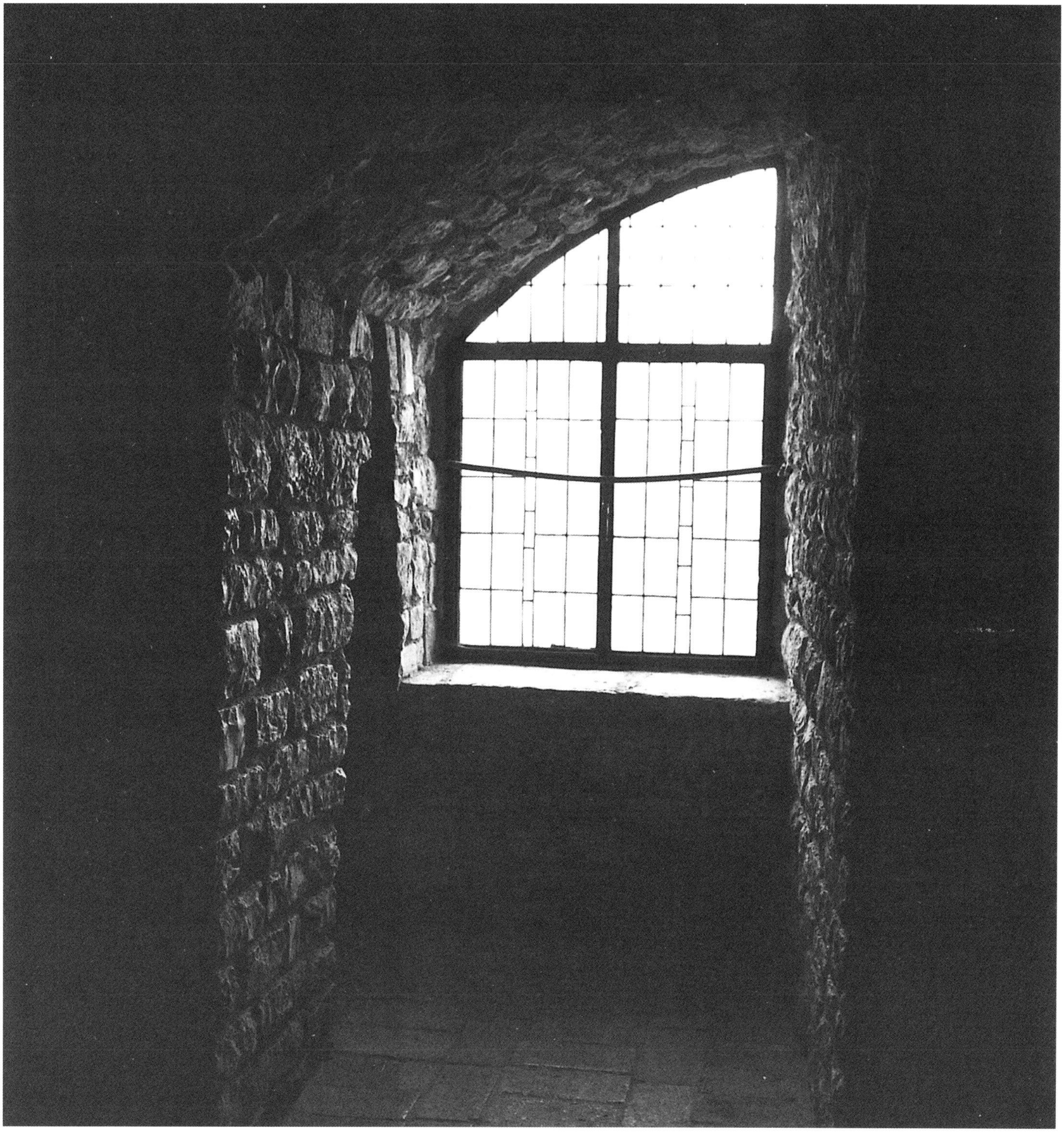

This transformation,

this divinization of humanity,

took place behind the columns of cloister.

There, in a grand reversal of a paradoxical God,

physical confinement was spiritual liberty.

Sanctified space enabled the community

to remain outside the cavern of greedy ambition

that was luring Assisi into its darkness.

———■———

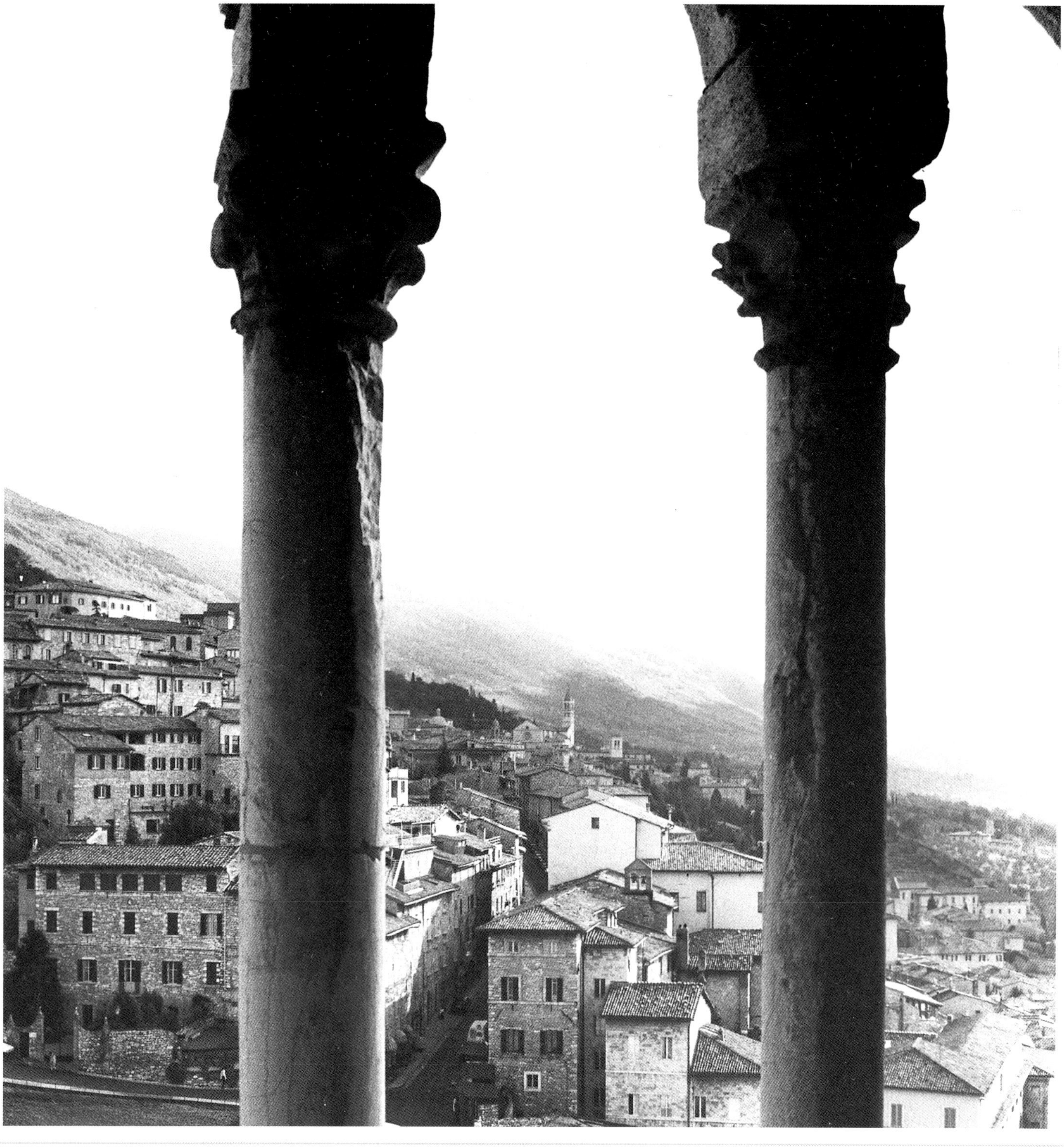

Dwelling in opulent emptiness below the town,

the Poor Ladies were guided by Lady Poverty herself

as they fashioned a home for Holiness.

Clare rejoiced in this sister whose lovely simplicity drew Christ near:

"O blessed poverty, who bestows eternal riches on those who

love and embrace her!

O holy poverty, God promises the kingdom of heaven and, in fact, offers eternal glory

and a blessed life to those who possess and desire you!

O God-centered poverty whom the Lord Jesus Christ

condescended to embrace before all else!"

———■———

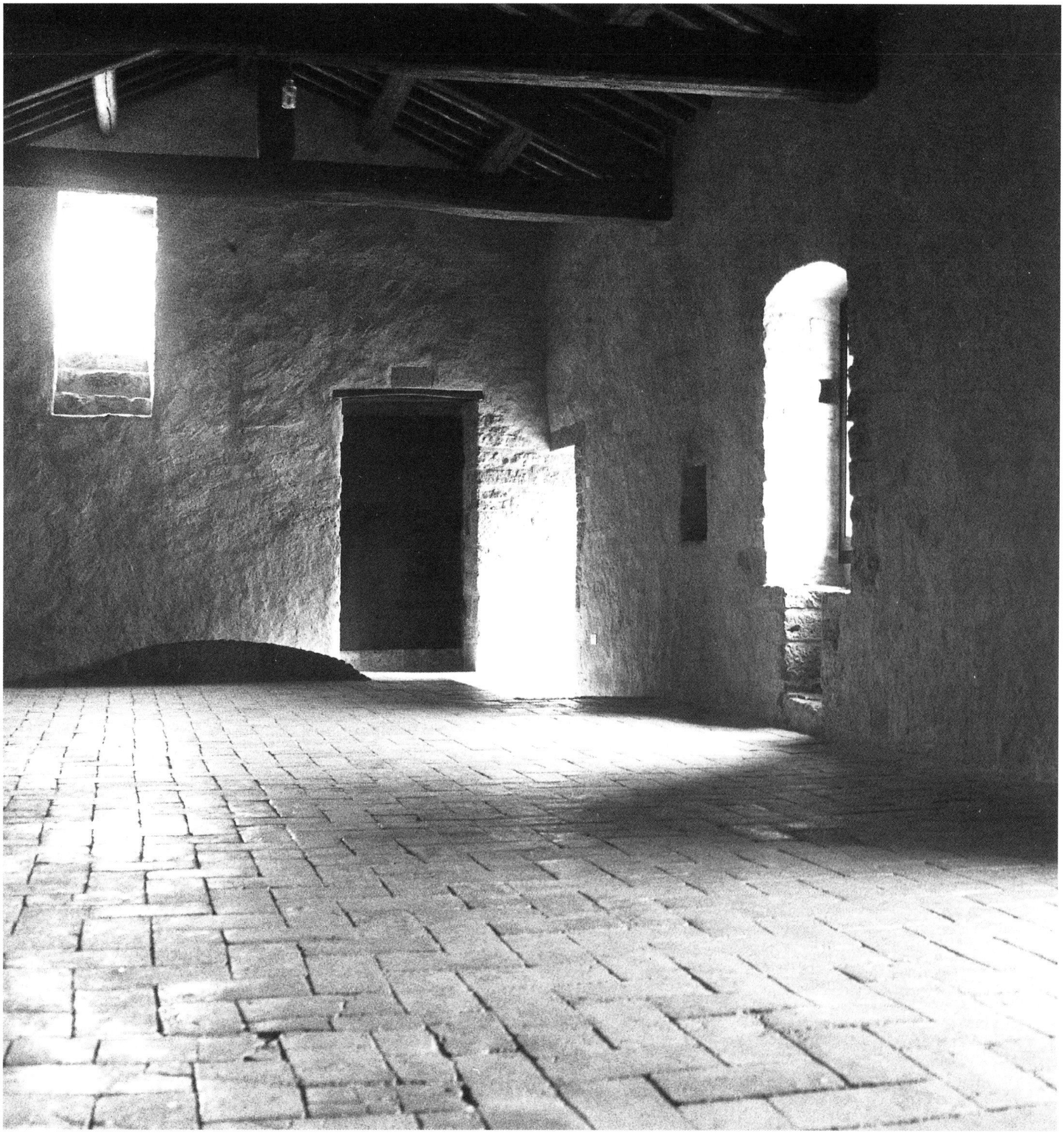

Lady Poverty challenged her sisters to be poor

not only in their household but also in their hearts.

Immersed in crucified Love, the holy women emptied themselves

after the example of Christ.

And, just as Jesus had conquered power through weakness,

Clare began to conquer domination through servitude.

She stooped from her nobility to wash the feet of the others,

including the servant women

who became her equals in the cloister.

———■———

13

Not long after beginning their unique cycle

of mutual service and silent contemplation,

the Poor Ladies achieved a fruitful union with the Lord of Creation.

Clare and her sisters conceived new life

as their withdrawal from destructive social norms

allowed them to cherish the entire Body of Christ.

Thus, the enclosure at San Damiano became

a womb for these Godbearers

who were following in the "footprints of the Virgin Mary."

───■───

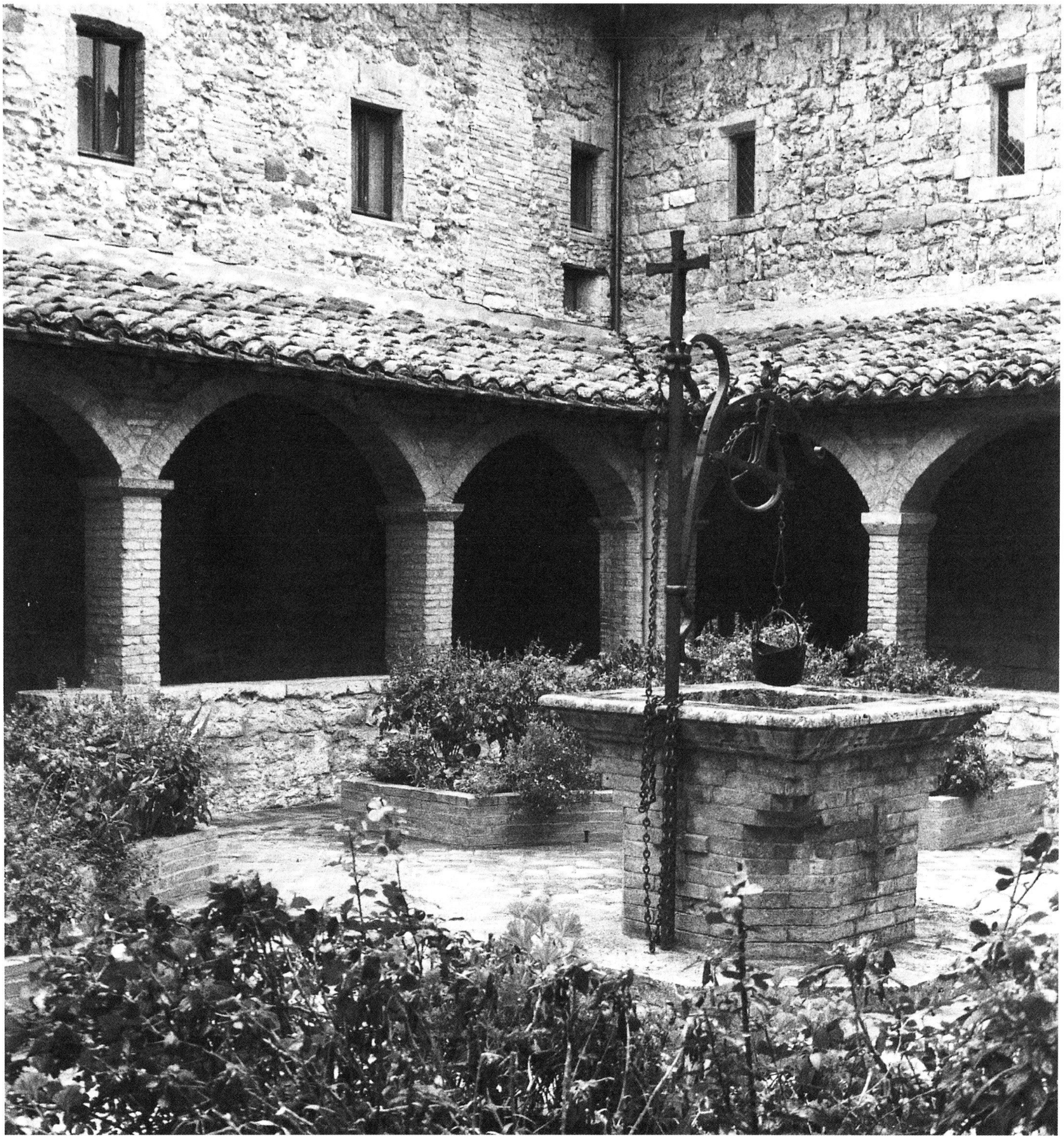

Like the Mother of God,

the virgin Clare and her sisters gave birth to Christ's humanity

for a people wandering far away from Divinity.

These spiritual mothers tenderly nursed

those hungering for Incarnate Love

by filling them with a comforting truth:

Jesus, who was born in time and raised in history,

who celebrated with friends and dined with sinners,

who worked in sweat and died in sacrifice,

was still fully alive in their midst.

———■———

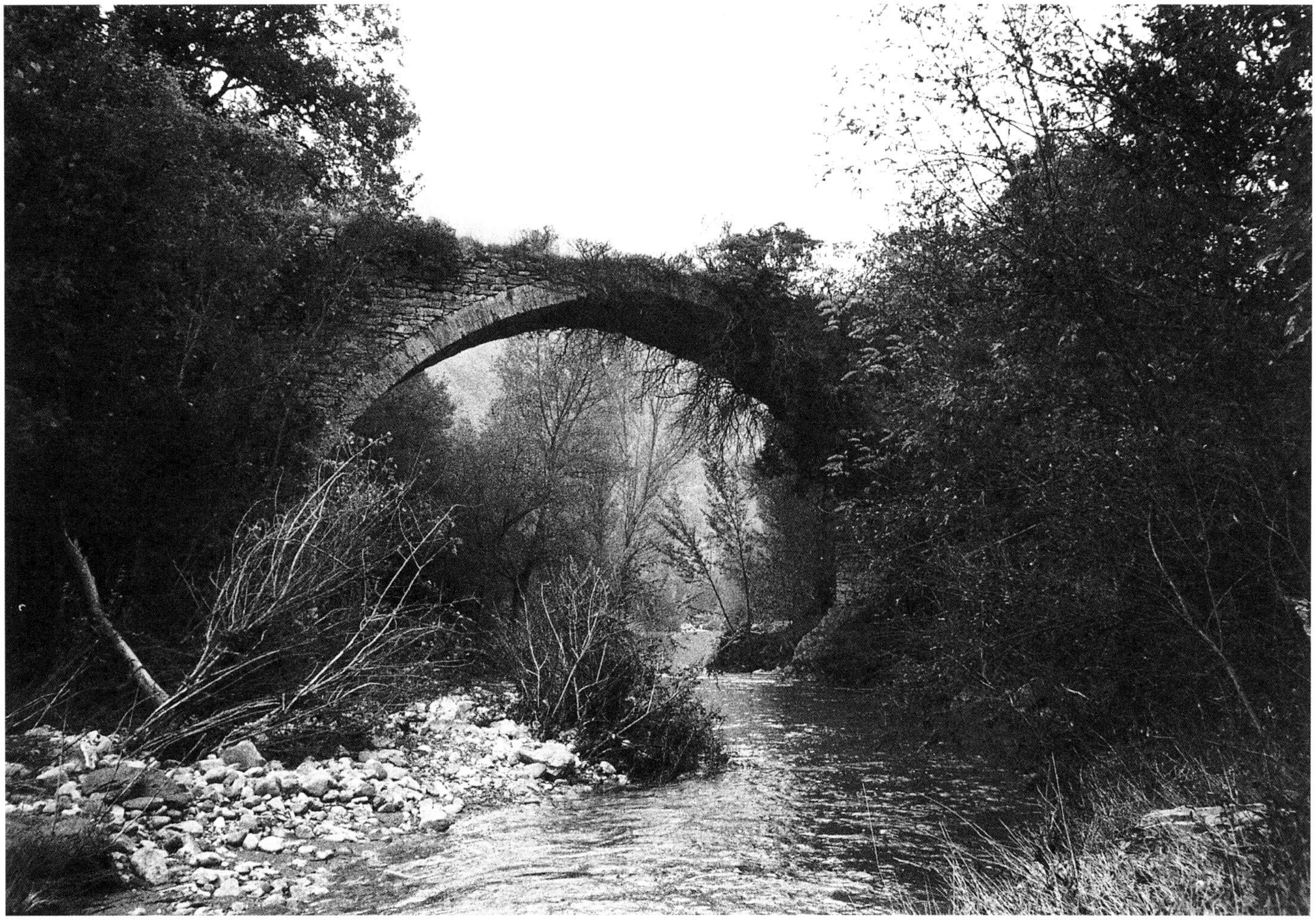

As maternal witnesses of Christ's abiding presence,

the Poor Ladies nurtured the feeble faith

of commoners, nobles and outcasts alike.

Recognizing their dignity as royal children of God,

Clare's community led the way to the land of Mercy

where even a peasant princess or a pauper prince

could delight in the fields of divine inheritance

and discover hope

in the abundant orchards of grace.

———■———

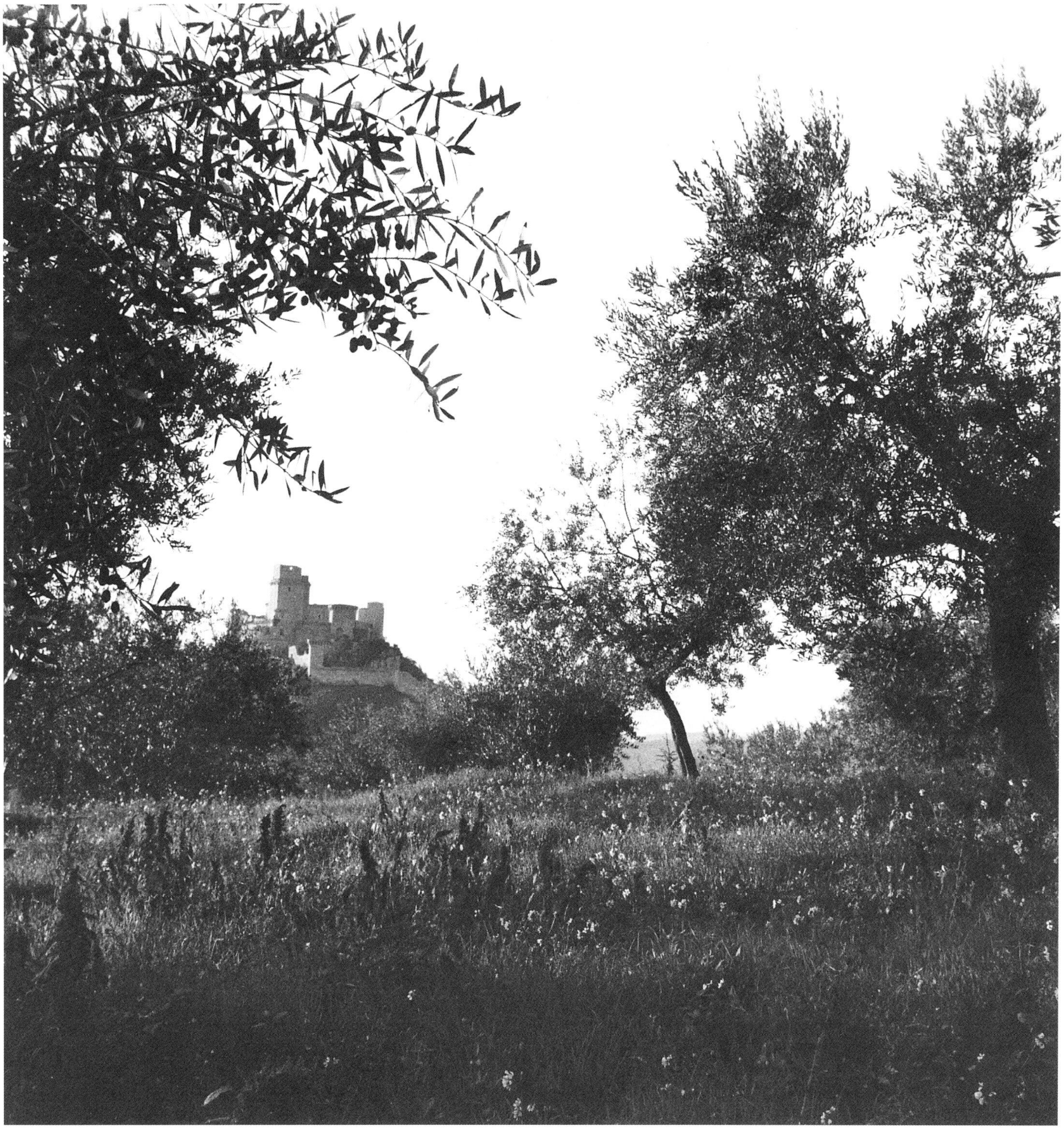

But royalty brought responsibility.

Clare taught her followers

that even though the rich bounty of God's grace

was freely given, it remained unharvested without human effort.

Grace, like the olive,

was meant to be gathered from willowy branches of Love

flourishing in rocky soil.

Once accepted, grace would be poured into the heavy press of daily life.

There Mercy flowed like the precious olive oil:

nourishing, illuminating, anointing and healing.

———■———

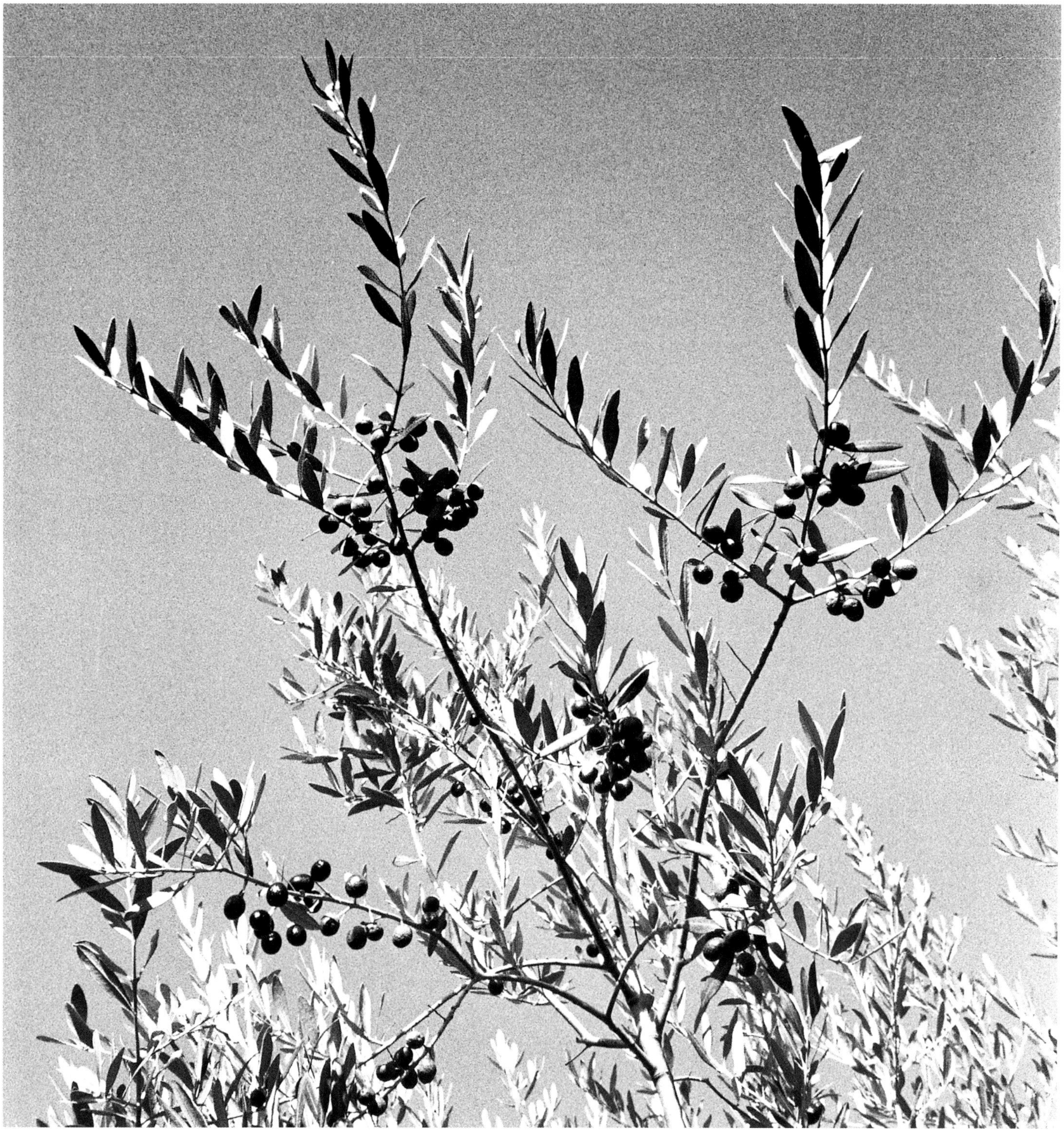

It was this marvelous balm of grace

that began to vivify the weary Church.

Divine initiative and human response.

Prayer and discipleship. Poor Ladies and Friars Minor. Women and men.

Together they formed the solid foundation

for a rebuilt house of God.

Clare and Francis directed the labor as they worked side by side

to raise sturdy walls of evangelical commitment.

Clare's steady hands cemented the living stones of the Gospel

that Francis zealously carried in the world.

———■———

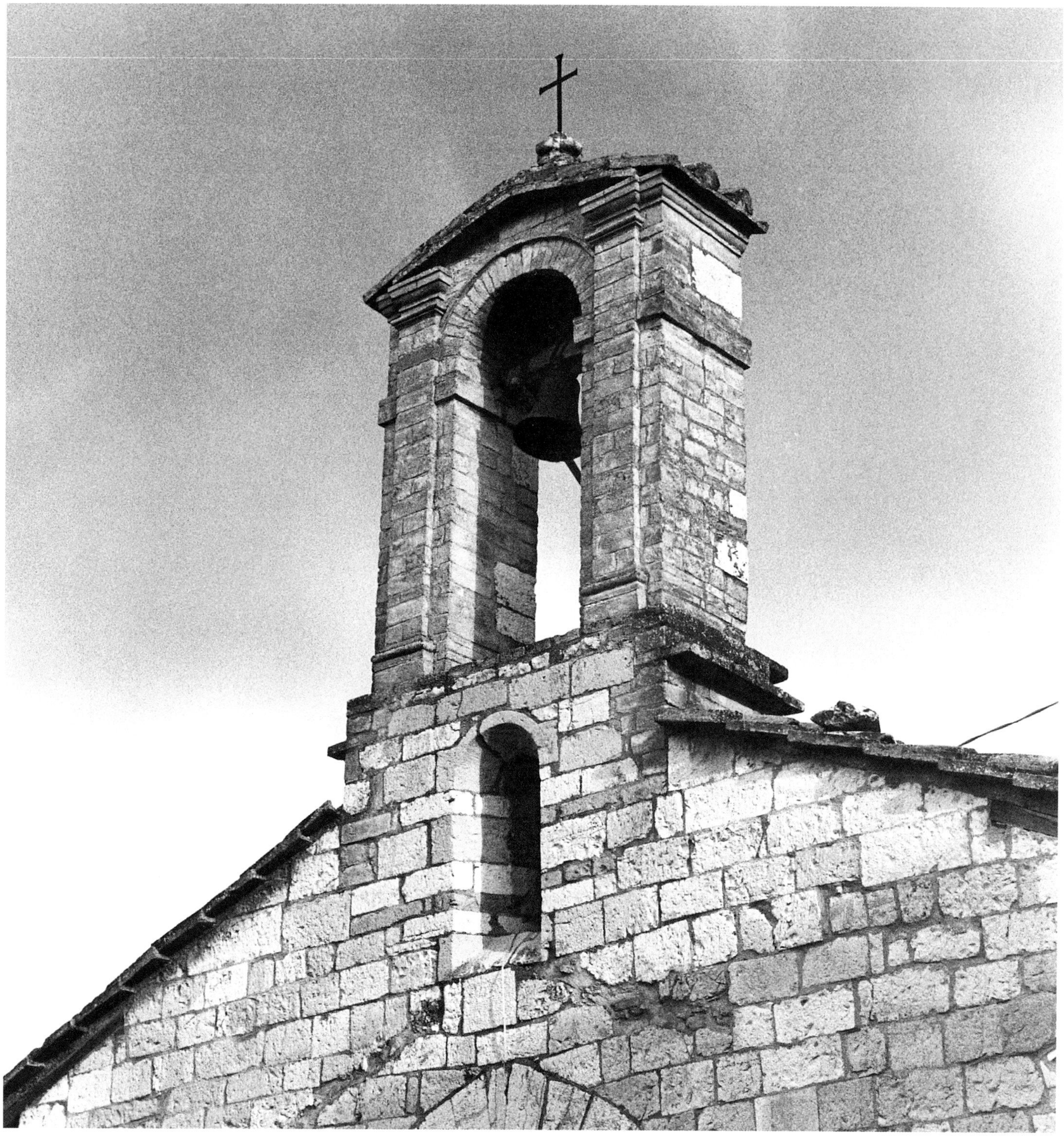

During this often frustrating and always exhausting work,
Clare and Francis found solace in their luminous friendship.
Francis edified Clare with his heartfelt preaching
and gifted her with an approved Form of Life.
In turn, Clare gently tended to Francis' wounded body and spirit
as his declining health and fractured brotherhood
plagued him with relentless pain.
Finally in 1226, after her dear friend embraced Sister Death,
Clare was left alone to carry the torch of divine inspiration
that had cast its brilliance upon their entwined destinies.

———■———

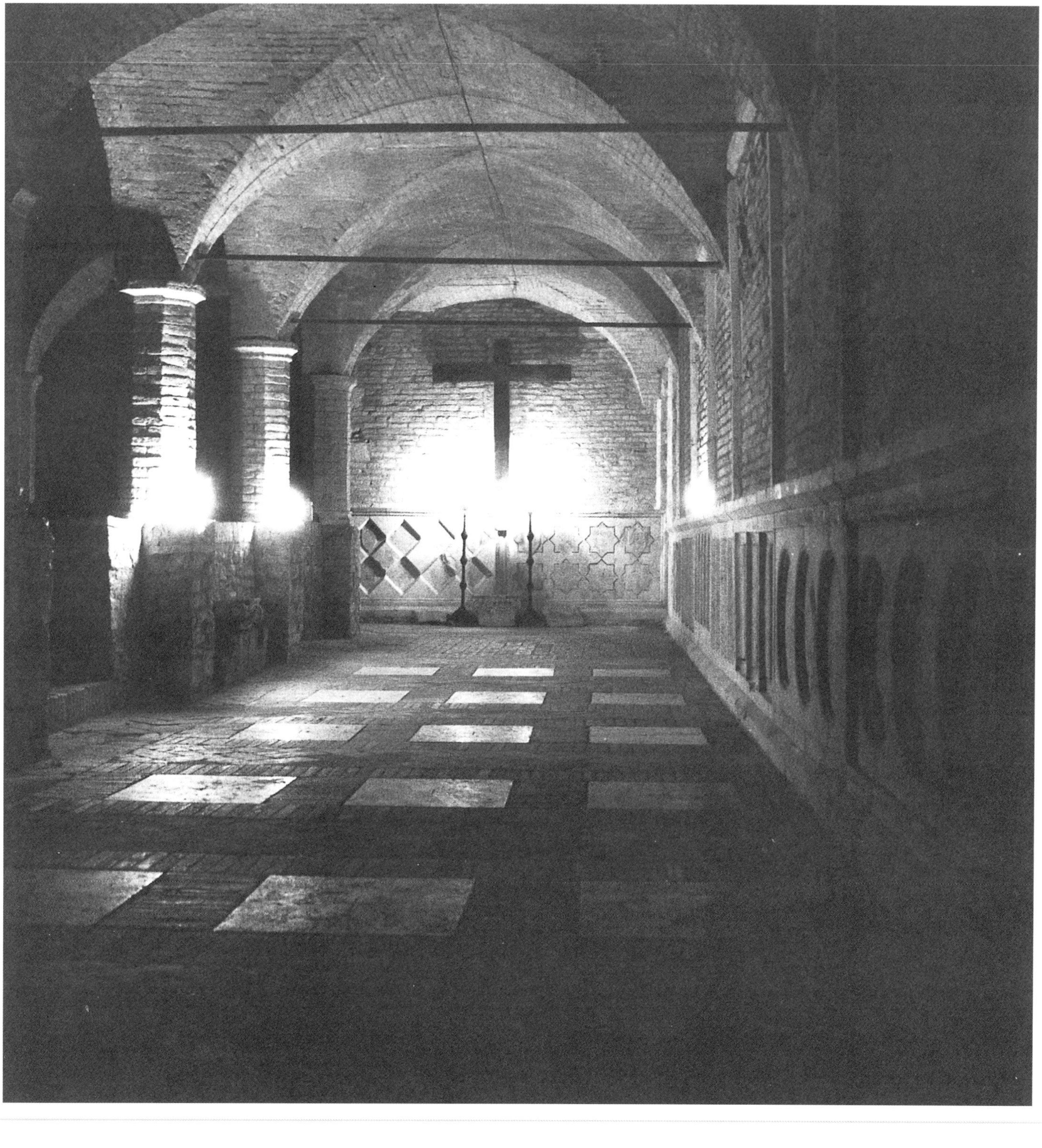

The seasons passed quickly now

and the verdant summer of Clare's life faded into autumn.

Eventually the rigors of penance pulled Clare into a bed of Passion

where she remained for almost twenty-nine years.

Suffering burnished Clare's wisdom

and prompted her to prescribe moderation for the other sisters.

"I beg you . . . dearly beloved, to refrain wisely and prudently

from an indiscreet and an impossible austerity in the fasting

you have undertaken. And I beg you in the Lord to praise the Lord

by your very life, to offer the Lord your reasonable service and

your sacrifice always seasoned with salt."

———■———

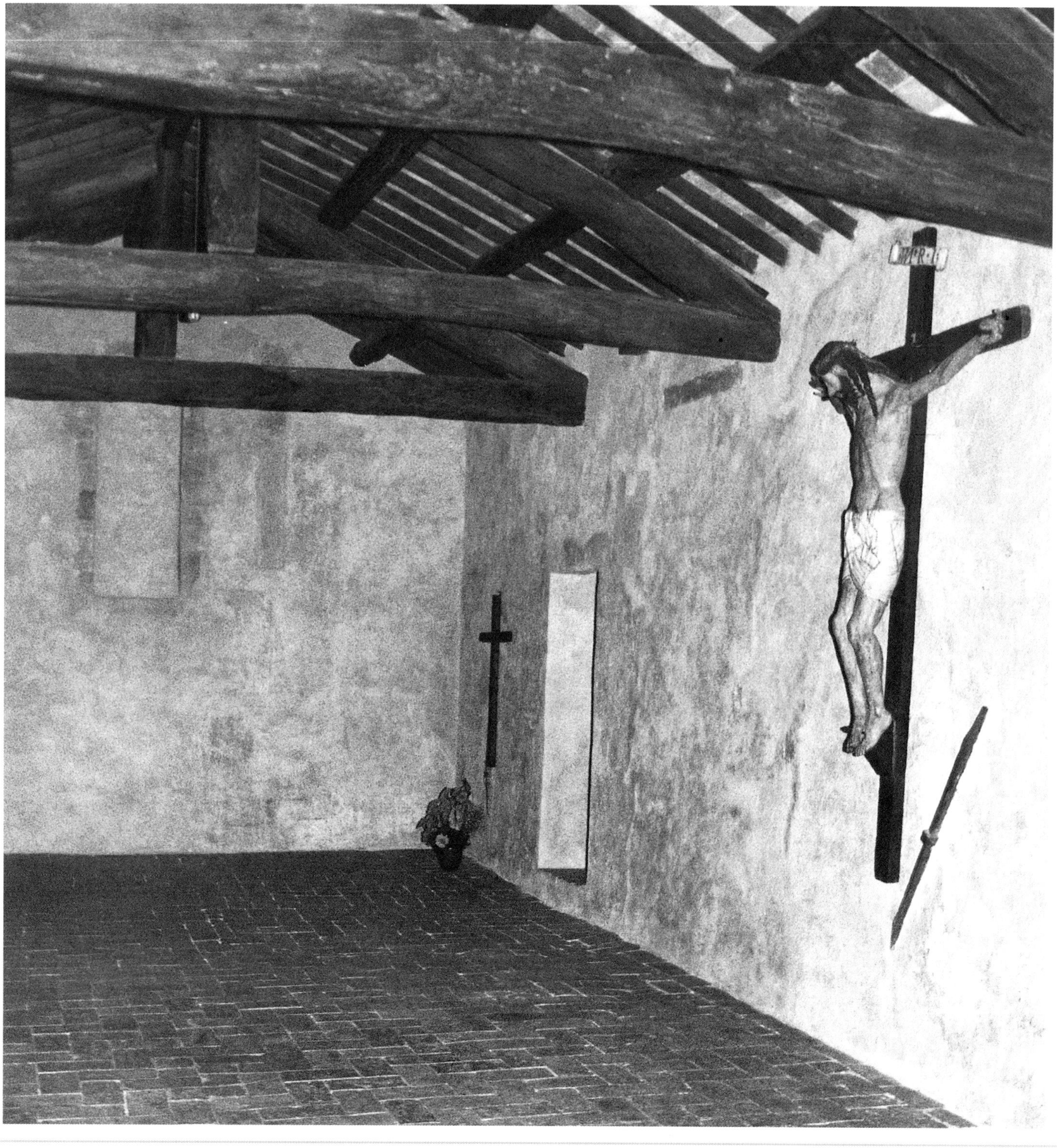

But even as Clare tempered her community's mortifications,

she clung tightly to Lady Poverty's hand.

Convinced that this pure sister led them to God,

Clare employed spiritual integrity and candid diplomacy

to safeguard the Privilege of Poverty

through the twists and turns of five papacies.

———■———

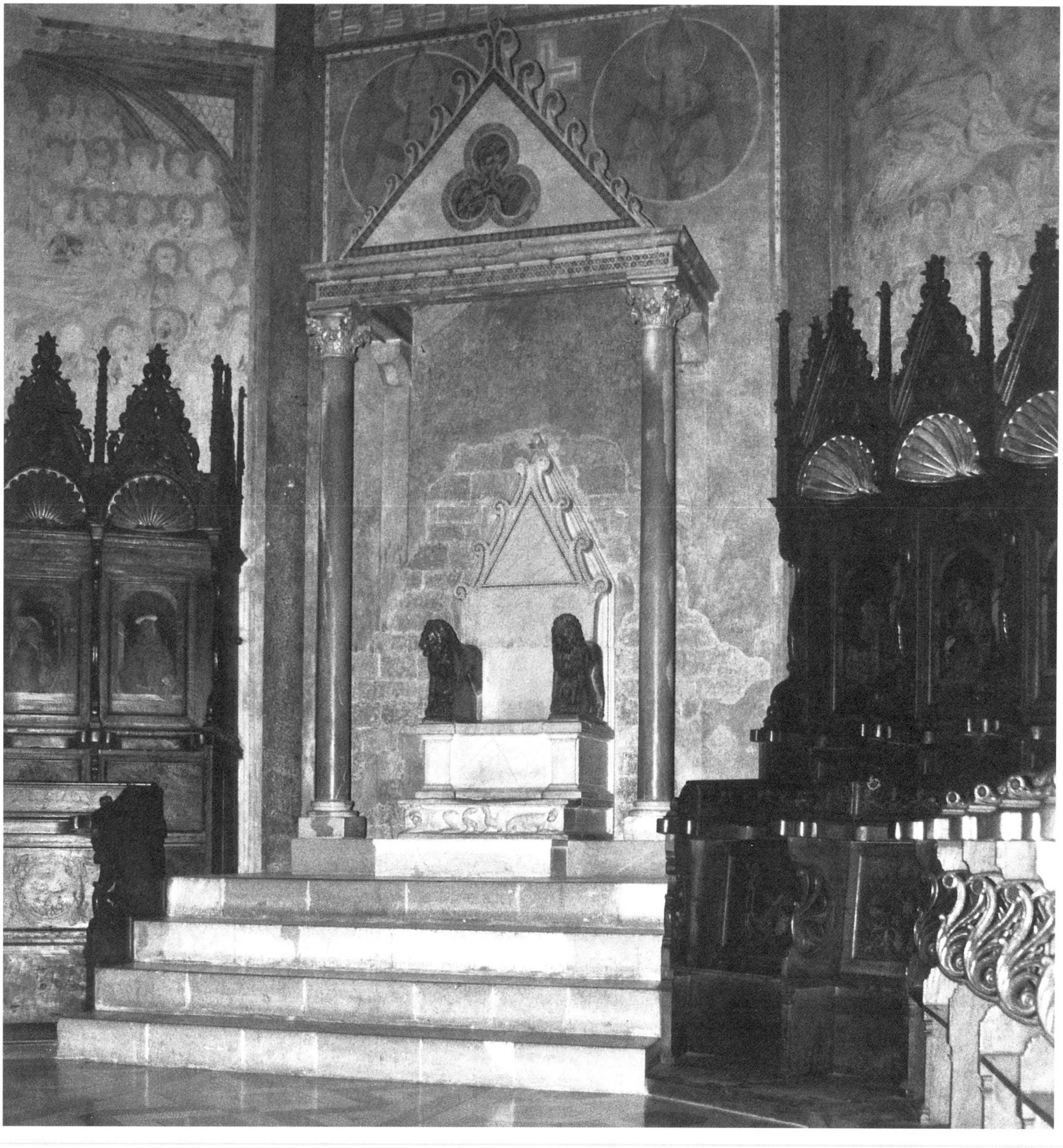

Recognizing that her earthly sojourn was near its end,

fifty-five year old Clare worked diligently

to protect the legacy of poverty for her sisters.

Love's watchful gaze encompassed this infirmed yet determined leader

as she began to write her own Rule of Life.

Over the next several years Clare skillfully designed a document

that combined the Privilege of Poverty

with the essential elements of previous Rules.

She submitted her Rule to Rome

and then waited for a response.

———■———

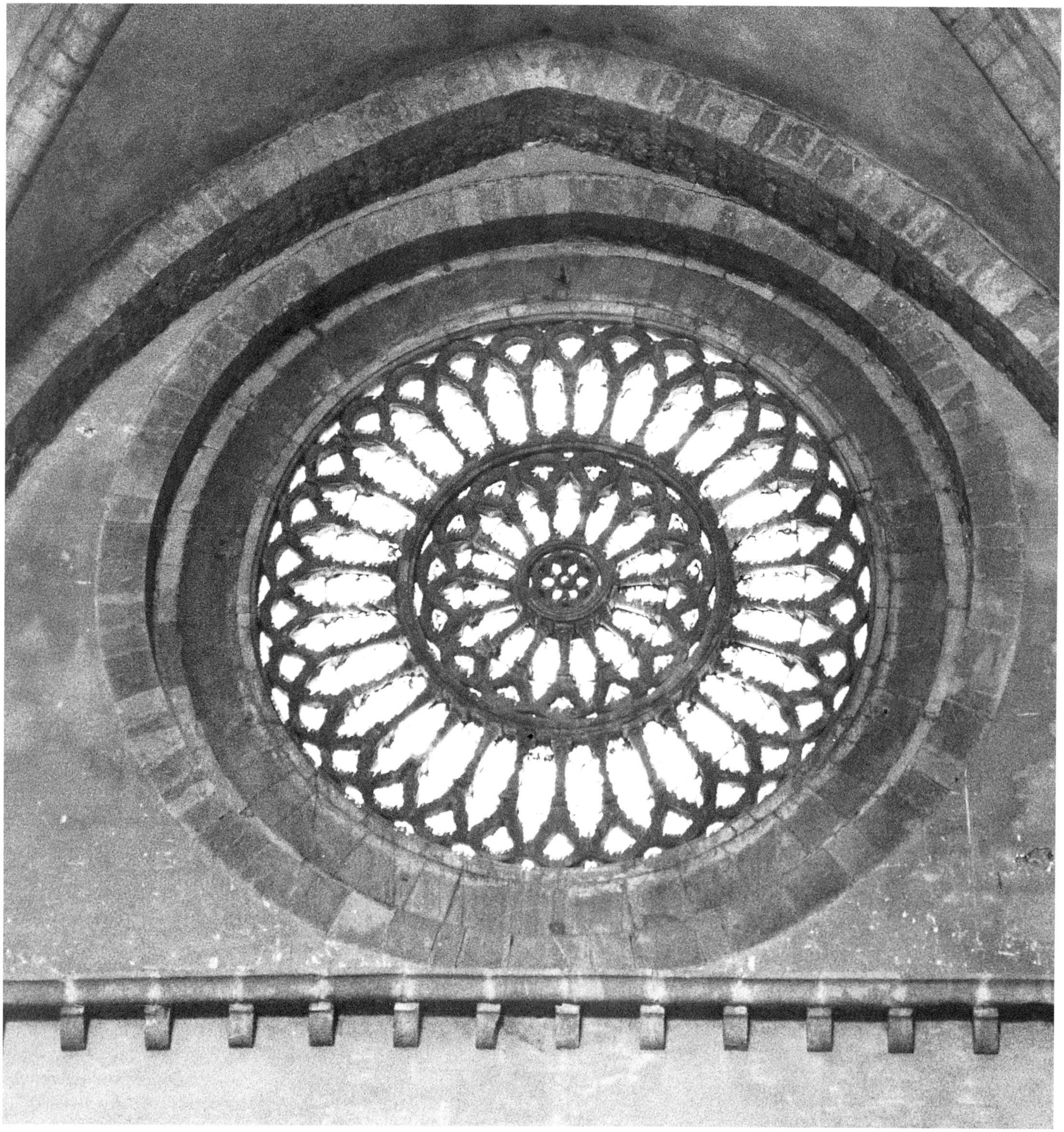

"So be it!"

These three words burst through the ranks of doubt and misunderstanding

that threatened to imprison Lady Poverty

in the lofty tower of impossible ideals.

"So be it!"

These three words sealed forever the blessed fate of the Poor Ladies

as Pope Innocent IV signed the Rule of Clare.

"So be it!"

These three words formed a hymn of praise as Clare

kissed again and again the first official religious Rule

written by a woman.

———■———

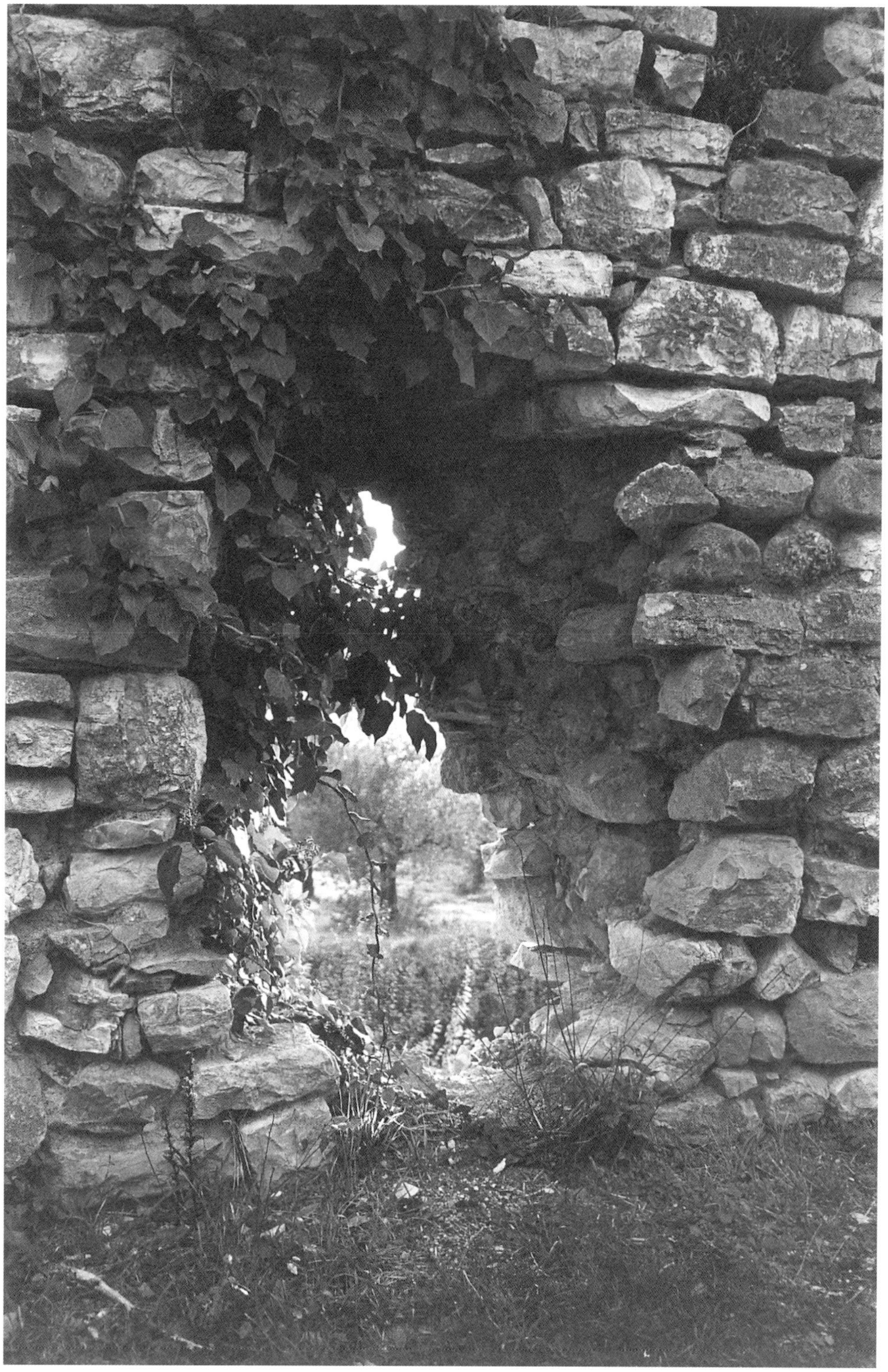

The next day
Clare's hymn of praise became a sigh of completion.

It was finished.

Her illustrious life entered its glorious culmination

as Clare breathed her last on August 11, 1253.

She left behind a world lashed by a storm of social turmoil,

yet a world renewed in hope,

a world still absorbing the rays of Love

that Clare of Assisi

had reflected for sixty years.

———■———

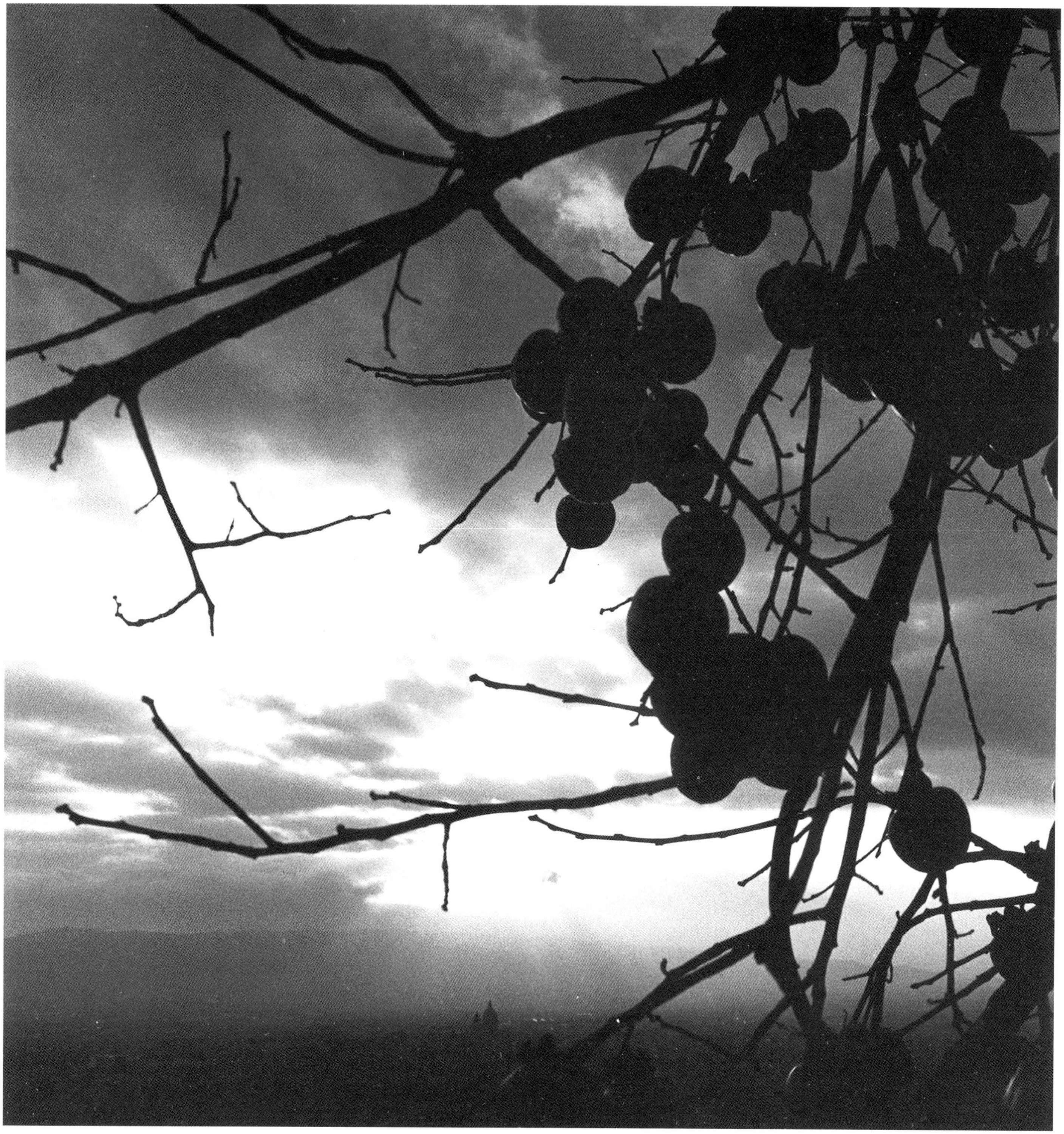

And the light continues to shine.

Saint Clare directs the beams of Mercy

toward the women who follow in her footprints

and toward all of us, her beloved Body of Christ:

"I bless you during my life and after my death, as I am able,

out of all the blessings with which the Father of mercies has

and does bless His sons and daughters in heaven and on earth. . . . Amen.

Always be lovers of your souls and those of all your sisters.

And may you always be eager to observe what you have promised the Lord.

May the Lord be with you and may you always be with the Lord. Amen."

———■———

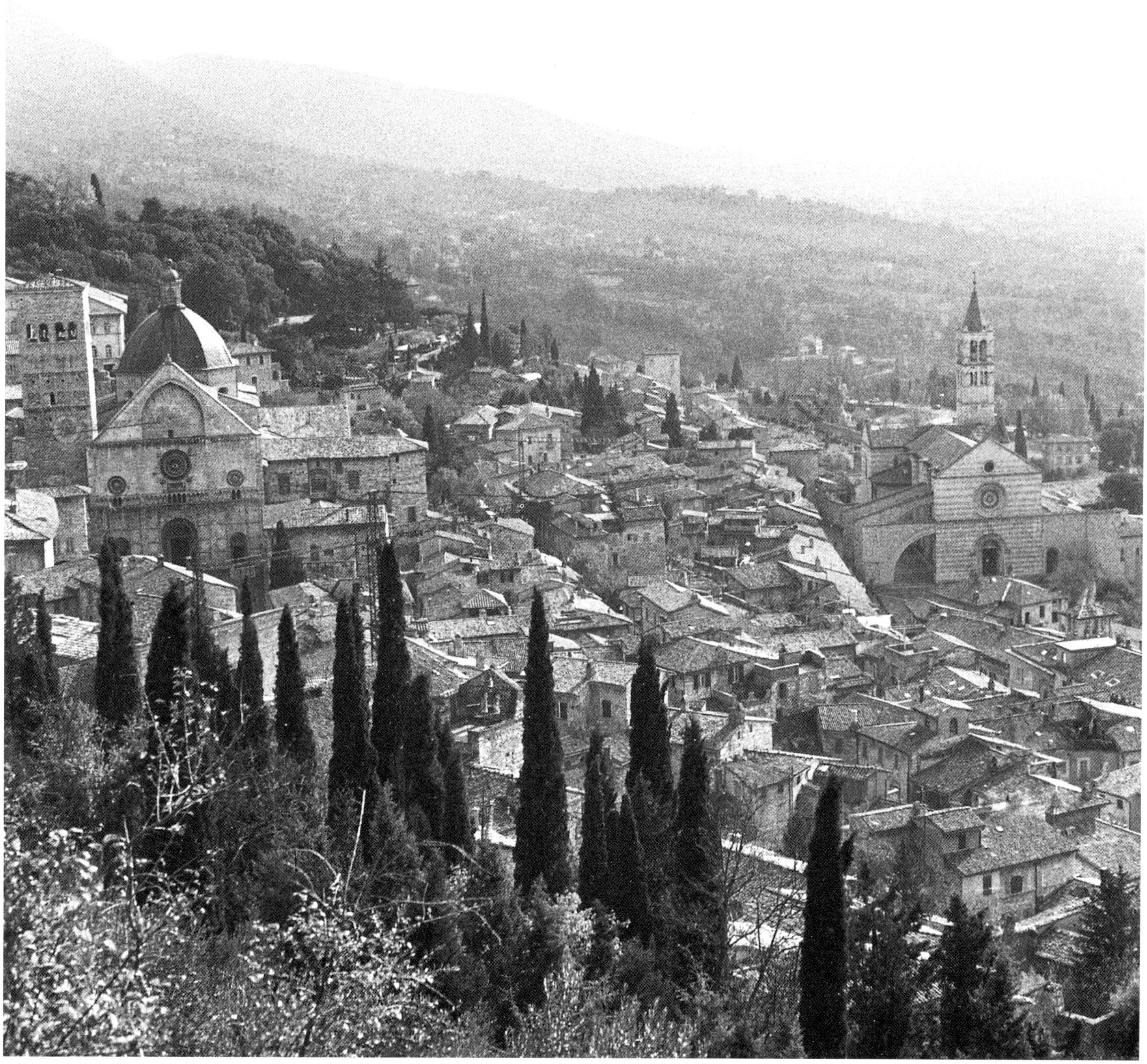

Photograph References

1. City of Perugia in the snow.
2. Basilica of Saint John Lateran, Rome, the center of Church government during the Middle Ages.
3. Remnants of a noblemen's medieval fortress, Rome.
   Ref: *The Acts of the Process of Canonization* (3.28).
   Ref: Ingrid J. Peterson, OSF, *Clare of Assisi, A Biographical Study*. (Quincy, IL: Franciscan Press, 1993) p. 43.
4. Street lamp in the main square of Assisi.
   Ref: Peterson, p. 1.
5. Crest of Perugia, a griffin attacking its prey.
6. Medieval manor, Perugia.
7. Fountain in the piazza of the Basilica of Saint Clare, Assisi.
8. Cathedral of San Rufino, Assisi. The manor house of Saint Clare is to the left.
9. Door of Saint Clare's family home.
10. Street in Assisi.
11. One of the city gates of Assisi.
12. Road between Assisi and the Portiuncula.
13. Crucifix in Saint Mary Major, the Cathedral of Assisi during Clare's lifetime, where both Francis and Clare were baptized.
14. Flying buttresses supporting the walls of the Basilica of Saint Clare.
15. Olive tree near the church of San Damiano.
16. Olive trees in the Umbrian countryside.
17. Porticato, a cloistered walkway, at the Basilica of Saint Francis.
    Ref: *Second Letter of Saint Clare to Saint Agnes of Prague* (1235) no. 21-22.

18. Dormitory window in the ancient section of the Sacro Convento, Assisi.
    Ref: *Third Letter of Saint Clare to Saint Agnes of Prague* (1238) no. 12-13.
19. View of Assisi from the bell tower of the Basilica of Saint Francis.
20. Clare's dormitory at San Damiano.
    Ref: *First Letter of Saint Clare to Saint Agnes of Prague* (1234) no. 15-17.
21. Clare's refectory at San Damiano.
22. Garden cloister at San Damiano.
    Ref: Peterson, p. 268.
23. Medieval bridge spanning the Tescio River in the forest below Assisi.
24. Rocca Maggiore, the imperial castle where the Duke of Spoleto governed Assisi and its environs.
25. Olive tree at harvest time, Assisi.
26. Bell tower of the Magdalene Chapel, the site of the leper colony where Francis and the early friars ministered.
27. Cloister cemetery, Basilica of Saint Francis.
28. Crucifix in the dormitory of San Damiano.
    Ref: *Third Letter of Saint Clare to Saint Agnes of Prague* (1238) no. 40-41.
29. Papal throne in the Basilica of Saint Francis.
30. Rose window, Basilica of Saint Clare.
31. Rupture in the ancient wall of the Rocca Minore, a watch tower for the castle of Assisi.
    Ref: Approval of the *Rule of Saint Clare*, Pope Innocent IV.
32. Sunset from the garden of the Basilica of Saint Francis.
33. View of Assisi, with both the Cathedral of San Rufino, where Clare's family home was located, and the Basilica of Saint Clare, where her body rests in eternity.
    Ref: *The Blessing of Saint Clare* (1253) no. 11-12; 14-16.

All quotes from Clare's writings are adapted from Regis Armstrong, OFM CAP. *Clare of Assisi: Early Documents* (Mawhah, N.J.: Paulist Press, 1988).

SAINT CLARE CHRONOLOGY

1193 Lady Clare is born to the noble family of Ortulana and Favarone di Offreduccio.

1199 Violent civil upheaval exiles the noble families of Assisi to Perugia, among them the family of Lady Clare.

1210 The cousin of Lady Clare, Rufino, becomes one of Francis' first followers. Clare begins to seek spiritual guidance from Francis.

1212 Palm Sunday, Lady Clare joins Francis and his community at the Portiuncula.

1215 Francis gives Clare and her followers a Rule of Life.

1224 After receiving the stigmata on Mount La Verna, Francis is nursed near the convent of San Damiano.

1226 October 3, Francis dies at the Portiuncula. His body is taken to San Damiano where Clare and her sisters offer one last farewell.

1240 Through the prayers of Clare, the Saracen mercenaries abandon their siege of Assisi.

1253 August 9, Clare receives the approval of her Rule.

1253 August 11, Clare dies at San Damiano.

1255 Pope Alexander IV canonizes Clare and commissions a church to be built in her honor.